Uncle John's THE HAUNTED OUTHOUSE

BATHROOM READER FOR KIDS ONLY!

by the Bathroom Readers' Institute

• • •

Bathroom Readers' Press
Ashland, Oregon

UNCLE JOHN'S THE HAUNTED OUTHOUSE BATHROOM READER® FOR KIDS ONLY

For information, write: The Bathroom Readers' Institute
P.O. Box 1117 Ashland, OR 97520
www.bathroomreader.com

Cover design by Jane Sheppard
Cover illustration by Scot Ritchie
Folio illustration by Patrick Merrell
"How to Talk to a Ghost" illustration
by Nicholas R. Halliday

ISBN-10: 1-60710-784-8 / ISBN-13: 978-1-60710-784-2

Library of Congress Cataloging-in-Publication Data
Uncle John's the haunted outhouse bathroom reader for kids only.
    pages cm
ISBN 978-1-60710-784-2 (pbk.)
1. Wit and humor, juvenile. 2. Curiosities and wonders--Juvenile literature. I. Bathroom Readers' Institute (Ashland, Or.) II. Title: Haunted outhouse bathroom reader for kids only.
 PN6166.U585 2013
 081.02'07--dc23
                                        2013010760

Printed in the United States of America
First Printing, 2013

17 16 15 14 13   6 5 4 3 2 1

READERS RAVE

. . . .

Some books print fancy reviews written by fancy book critics. Borrring! At the BRI, we care more about what our faithful readers have to say.

"This book is the best book in the world I've ever read, since now I've read it!"

—Trevor G.

"I inadvertently stole one from my teacher. (Sorry Mr. Mont!) I got hooked, my family got hooked, and now I have my nieces and nephews hooked!"

—Michael C.

"I remember reading the first *Bathroom Reader* as a kid, and learning that Barbie had a last name. (Roberts!)"

—Katie F.

"I love your books! I have eleven books. I take them to school and everyone loves to read them. "

—Andrew S.

"Waassssuuuupppp! I just wanted to shout out to all the cool dudes and chicas working on the Bathroom Reader staff! I became totally addicted to the BRs last year! My life hasn't been the same since!"

—Kim B.

THANK YOU

· · · · · · · · · · · · · · · · · · · ·

The Bathroom Readers' Institute sincerely thanks the people whose advice and assistance made this book possible.

Gordon Javna

Kim T. Griswell

Trina Janssen

Jay Newman

Brian Boone

Jane Sheppard

Scot Ritchie

Rich Wallace

Carly Schuna

Jahnna Beecham

Kelly Milner Halls

Mark Haverstock

Elizabeth Armstrong Hall

Molly Marcot

Megan Todd

Sandra Neil Wallace

Nancy Coffelt

Valeri Gorbachev

John O'Brien

Will Strong

Michelle R. Weaver

Patrick Merrell

Nick Halliday

Joan M. Kyzer

Jill Belrose

Carly Stephenson

Melinda Allman

Blake Mitchum

Brandon Walker

JoAnn Padgett

Aaron Guzman

Ginger Winters

Jennifer Frederick

RR Donnelley

Publishers Group West

Thomas Crapper

TABLE OF CONTENTS

· ·

THAT'S BEASTLY!

BARFARAMA!

CREEPY CRAWLERS

MAD SCIENCE

TERRA SCARA

GET SPOOKED!

A tree! Go right! Uhn-n-n? A tree! Go left!

Find out what happens on page 53.

CHILLING GREETINGS

· · · · · · · · · · · · · · · · · · · ·

NOT LONG AGO, in a little red house with creaking doors and strange smells coming from the bathroom, we created an enchanting book of magic, mystery, science, history, and totally twisted tales. It's called *The Enchanted Toilet.* It's packed with amazing stories about castles and kingdoms and fairies and knights…but, I digress. The book you have in your hands is NOT filled with glitter glue and magic and Elvis impersonators (sorry, no time to fill you in…). Oh, no, my reading friends. *This* book began with a lightning bolt, a crash of thunder, and—*bwa ha ha!*—a rubber duckie.

One dark and stormy night, while I was writing the flesh off my fingers, a strange noise came from the front porch of the Bathroom Readers' Institute. I opened the door and saw…nothing really. But as I started to close the door, something so weird, so horrifying, so completely unbelievable waddled out of the shadows and said…

IT'S TIME TO TELL MY STORY . . .

Who was I to refuse? I invited the creature in, said "Stop looking at my neck like that!" and took down its ghastly tale (see page 99). And that's when I realized: My pointy-toothed visitor couldn't be the only monster with an eerily twisted history. I would find more stories about gruesome creatures and creepy ghosts and sewer pipes that go bump in the night! Then I'd stitch them all together to create a terror-filled book called...*The Haunted Outhouse.*

HOLD ON TO YOUR NECK BOLTS!

Flip through the pages of this *Uncle John's Bathroom Reader for Kids Only* and you'll find headless ghosts, haunted schools, bouncing eyeballs, severed hands, foods too icky to eat, history's most terrifying tyrants, and the U.S. government's advice for surviving a zombie apocalypse. You'll also find more than a dozen eerily twisted tales of horror, *plus* fourteen illustrated graphic horror tales. Every page is guaranteed to make your knees knock together no matter where you sit down to read.

By the way, that annoying little monster smelling up the pages? That's Count Fartula. If anything in this book really stinks—the jokes, for example—it's his fault. We think he's the fart fairy's second cousin twice-removed (see *The Enchanted Toilet*). I asked the fart fairy to magic him out of the book, but she refused, so I turned him into a game: "Find Count Fartula." To play, simply count how many times he appears in the book. Then turn to page 285 and discover your reward. (No peeking, or I'll send Count Fartula to stink up *your* house. Pee-uw!)

May all your outhouses be haunted...

Go with the flow!

UNCLE JOHNENSTEIN

THAT'S ZOMEDY!

· ·

A few laughs from the undying art of zombie comedy.

Q: What do you get when you cross a zombie with a snowman?
A: Frostbite.

Q: Do zombies eat candy with their fingers?
A: No, they eat the fingers separately.

Q: Where's the safest room in your house to hide from zombies?
A: The living room.

Q: What did the zombie eat after his teeth were cleaned?
A: The dentist.

Q: Why did the zombie take a nap?
A: He was dead tired.

Q: What did the zombie say when he saw his favorite movie star?
A: "I've been dying to eat you!"

ZOMBIE KID: "Mommy, do I have Daddy's eyes?"
MOMBIE: "Yes, dear. Now eat them before they get too cold."

Q: What's dead, flies around, and likes to sting your brain?
A: A zom-bee.

"Knock knock."
"Who's there?"
"Interrupting Zombie."
"Interrupting Zom-"
"BRAAAINS!"

IN THE NEWS

· · · · · · · · · · · · · · · · · · · ·

Truth really is stranger than fiction.

SPIDER INSIDE HER

Put this one at the top of your nightmare list: A Chinese woman, only known as "Ms. Lee," went to China's Changsha Central Hospital, complaining of an itchy ear. When Dr. Liu Sheng took a look inside, he found…a spider living in the woman's ear canal. Apparently it had crawled in while Lee was asleep. The doctor feared that extracting the spider with surgical equipment might cause it to drill its barbs deeper. So she washed the spider out with a saline solution.

COLOR ME YELLOW

A roadkill-raccoon got an extra stripe when a Pennsylvania road crew painted a yellow traffic line over its corpse. A biker who came across the roadkill thought the foul-up was some kind of joke. "When I saw it, I almost wrecked my motorcycle I was laughing so hard," he said. It was no joke: The Pennsylvania Department of Transportation usually has a clean-up vehicle ahead of a paint truck to clear debris—and dead raccoons. But on that day, no truck was available. The striped racoon has since been cleaned up, but a foot-long gap remains where "Old Yeller" used to be.

FEAR FACTOIDS

....

Proof that there's nothing to fear but stupidity itself.

• In 1990, members of a Congressional subcommittee wanted to know more about computer terrorism so they could come up with ways to fight it. The committee's research included watching *Die Hard 2*.

• In 2002, the *New York Times* reported a rumor about Bakili Muluzi, the president of the African country of Malawi. Muluzi had been accused of colluding with vampires to collect human blood for international aid agencies. Villagers believed the rumor. They stoned one man to death for "helping vampires" and attacked three Catholic priests they suspected of vampirism.

• A black leopard caused mass panic in Xiamen City, China in 2007. The beast was spotted on a busy downtown sidewalk. "Dogs were scared and passersby were running for their lives," said one observer. "Some of them ran into traffic, causing a backup." Police brought in a specialist from the local zoo to put the animal to sleep so it could be captured. But after watching for awhile, officers noticed something odd: the leopard never moved. One daring officer went up and touched it. That's when he realized it wasn't a real leopard. It was a stuffed *toy* leopard.

I'LL NEVER THROW UP!

· ·

An Uncle John's Eerily Twisted Tale!

PETER PAN WAS THE ODDEST EATER at Lost Bay
Elementary in Lost Bay, Connecticut. He could eat
anything. When he ate an entire pumpkin, all the boys
chanted, "Peter, Peter, pumpkin eater." But teasing only
encouraged Peter. Pretty soon, he was shoving anything
into his mouth on a dare. The Lost boys brought Peter
silverware, plates, and small appliances. Peter gobbled
them up. They brought lawn furniture, discarded
treadmills, and their little sisters' Big Wheels. Peter
gulped them down. And, unbelievably, it all stayed down.

"You keep eating all that junk and you're going to
throw up," warned Peter's big sister, Wendy.

Peter put his hands on his hips and declared, "I
won't throw up. I won't throw up."

But, one day, Peter went too far. He ate his entire
neighborhood—houses, sidewalks, street lamps, and
streets. He spared the people, mostly because they got
in their cars and screeched away (leaving no forwarding
addresses). And that's how Peter and the Lost boys ended
up with no moms or dads or sisters and no place to live.

Peter invited the Lost Boys to a tire roast beside
Lost Bay. No one sat too close to the campfire. Partly
because the smell of roasting tires made them gag, and

partly because of the rumor that Peter had eaten the hand off a pirate who now had to wear a hook.

"I know I said I'd never, never throw up," Peter told the boys. "But I created our problem, and throwing up may be the only way to fix it. Do you believe I can do it?"

"Yes!" the boys cried. "We believe!"

"If you believe," Peter said. "Then clap your hands."

The Lost boys clapped and clapped. And soon they heard a rumbling that sounded as if it came from a distant star. (The second star to the right, actually.) The rumbling grew louder and louder until—at long last— Peter threw up. Bricks and gates and small appliances and weather vanes and finger bones and street lamps gushed out of his mouth and poured into Lost Bay. When the whole mess settled, it had become an island filled with odd-shaped trees and unusual little houses and wondrous play structures.

"Our own island!" the boys cried. "What should we call it?"

Peter shrugged. "How about Never Never Land?"

"That sounds like an amusement park," said Stinky Bell, the smallest and smelliest of the boys.

"It can be whatever we want it to be," said Peter. "And we can do whatever we want."

And that's how Peter Pan and the Lost boys came to live at Never Never Land, the happiest place on Earth, next to Disneyland, of course, but that's another story.

THE END

WHAT'S IN YOUR SUITCASE?

······················

*Get caught with any of these at airport security,
and it could be an open-and-shut case.*

A TIGER CUB. During a bag scan, staff at a Bangkok airport saw an object that looked a lot like a real animal on their x-ray images. Officers from livestock and wildlife departments were called in to open and inspect the bag. What they found inside? Stuffed tiger toys *and* a live—though sedated—two-month-old tiger cub.

BARBIE. When airlines can't find the owners of unclaimed luggage, they send the luggage to the Unclaimed Baggage Center in Scottsboro, Alabama. People can visit the Center and buy the items that were found. A woman bought a Barbie doll for her daughter at the Center. The daughter pulled the head off the Barbie doll, and $500 in rolled bills fell out of the doll's body– plenty of cash for a night on the town with Ken.

A SEAL'S HEAD. A biology professor flying from Boston's Logan International Airport to Denver had the severed head of a harbor seal in his luggage. He told airport security officers that he'd found a dead seal on a beach and cut off its head to use for "educational purposes." Not good. And not legal. Federal laws make it illegal to remove body parts from a dead mammal. And transporting wildlife body parts? Don't even think about it unless you have a permit. The professor didn't. If charged, he could be fined up to $20,000 and spend a year in prison.

GI JOE. Authorities at Los Angeles International Airport confiscated a semiautomatic rifle, but not from a GI…from a GI Joe action figure. Seems the action figure was packing heat—a tiny plastic replica rifle— that technically fell under the ban on carrying weapon replicas onto a plane. The English woman who was carrying the doll was surprised that the officials were taking it so seriously. "Security examined the toy as if it was going to shoot them," she said.

A FROZEN TURKEY. Most people put a change of clothes and a few personal items in their hand luggage. In December 2010, one passenger packed in a 10 lb. frozen turkey. The man was headed to Malaga, Spain, for Christmas and was worried that he would not be able to buy a turkey for Christmas dinner. Too bad: the frozen bird showed up in a scan of his hand luggage and was confiscated by security. It seems perishable goods cannot be transported abroad without permission. Deprived of his Christmas treat, the man reportedly said, "Why are you making a fuss—will it thaw at thirty thousand feet?"

WHAT'S THAT IN YOUR HAIR?

························

These people give new meaning to the phrase "bad hair day."

HAT GAG

Lady Gaga made a name for herself as the queen of celebrity style strangeness. And her hair is no exception. She wore a meat dress to the 2010 MTV Video Music Awards. But it's the slab of raw sirloin she wore as a hat that really makes us shudder. For those who wonder how Gaga's hair smelled at the end, the outfit's designer, Franc Fernandez, claimed it probably wasn't that bad. "It's actually very clean meat," said Fernandez. "It had a sweet smell. It hadn't been sitting out for more than five hours."

ELVIS HAS LEFT THE . . . HAIR

Actor Russell Brand prefers his animal fashion accessories to be alive. In his hair: a mouse. "Elvis—that was his name," Brand said in an interview with the BBC. "He lived there for about a month." According to Brand, he bought Elvis with the intention of keeping him in his hair indefinitely. "I just thought it would be nice to have him there," he said. The only time Brand ran into problems was at night. "He had a Tupperware box he occupied when I had to sleep."

FEATHERS AND FINS

When celebs like Hilary Duff, Ke$ha, Miley Cyrus, and Steven Tyler from *American Idol* started wearing feather extensions in their hair, they started a trend. That affected...the fly-fishing industry. Here's the thing: women started going to fly-fishing shops to find feathers. "It takes years and years and years to develop chickens to grow these feathers," said the assistant manager of one shop. "Now, instead of ending up on a fly, they're going into women's hair." Regular customers can find themselves out of luck when a store's entire stock of chicken feathers has ended up in women's hair. "A lot of people are peeved about it," said the manager. (But we're guessing the fish are pleased.)

MO-HAWKING HEALTH FOOD

Gasmy Joseph—nicknamed Mohawk—from Pompano Beach, Florida, found a way to earn cash with his Mohawk hairdo. It all started when a buddy asked Gaz to spray-paint a message on his hair to spread the word about his birthday party. Now, Gaz sells ad space on his high-standing hair. His clients include Deliver Lean, a health-food catering company. The company paid Gaz to spray-paint its logo on his Mohawk and walk around at Miami Heat and Florida Panthers games. "It's been tremendous marketing," said the company's founder. "It's great exposure, and it's never been done before."

•   •   •

WHO'S HAUNTING WHO?

·····················

Some say ghosts are dead people who don't know they're dead. They're still hanging around the same old places, so how could they be dead? It's not logical...but this puzzle is.

FOUR FRIENDS have accepted a challenge to spend the night in the creepy old Miller Mansion. Craig, Tyler, Jake, and Drew will win a big reward if they can endure the night, but each must stay alone in a bedroom until dawn. And the Miller Mansion is haunted...by four seriously angry ghosts. It's past midnight, and the ghosts—Henry, Patrick, Lucy, and the Butler—want to see and be seen. Use these 10 clues to figure out which ghost is haunting each boy.

1. The Butler was serving dinner in 1877 when little Henry said his first word: "vomit."

2. Jake's room is the only room in the attic.

3. Lucy and Henry were twins.

4. In 1893, 10-year-old Patrick was killed by poison.

5. Craig did not choose the gray room.

6. The ghost in the red room can be heard crying for his cat.

7. The oldest ghost was stabbed to death in 1939 in the yellow room, which he haunts.

8. The youngest ghost throws books in the gray room, which is across the hall from the blue room.

9. The ghost in Drew's room died peacefully, but she's been restless ever since.

10. The Butler never goes higher than the second floor.

Need a hint? First figure out which ghost is the oldest and which is the youngest. Where does that lead you? **Need another hint?** Make a chart like the one below. List the four boys, then the four room colors. Make a second chart for the ghosts and the rooms. As you read clues, X out the boxes that the clues rule out. (We've filled in Clue 5 to get you started.

BOYS	RED	YELLOW	GRAY	BLUE
CRAIG			X	
TYLER				
JAKE				
DREW				

GHOSTS	RED	YELLOW	GRAY	BLUE
HENRY				
PATRICK				
LUCY				
BUTLER				

Answers on page 285.

VILLAINESSES

· ·

Sometimes movie bad guys aren't guys at all!

VILLAINESS: Cruella de Vil, *101 Dalmatians* (1961)
HOW BAD IS SHE? Subtract the *la* from Cruella, you get *cruel*, and de + vil = *devil*. Rich and spoiled, this cruel devil loves her collection of fur coats more than anything. In the movie, she's on a single-minded mission to obtain fur for a black-and-white-spotted coat. Only one animal has white fur with black spots: the Dalmatian. Cruella's dastardly plan? Kidnap and skin Dalmatian *puppies* to make the coat.

VILLAINESS: Ursula, *The Little Mermaid* (1989)
HOW BAD IS SHE? This movie "bad girl" is a half-octopus half-human sea witch who's been cast out of the undersea kingdom by the mermaid's father, King Triton. Ursula wants revenge and she gets it by making a devilish bargain with the mermaid. Ursula will transform Ariel into a human for three days. If she can win the heart of the human prince she loves, all will be well. But if not? Ariel will become Ursula's slave. To seal the bargain, the mermaid must hand over her beautiful singing voice. The tricky Ursula then uses Ariel's voice to snag the prince herself. When her scheme is uncovered, Ursula conjures up a storm at sea to kill Ariel and her prince. But her

villainy backfires—she's impaled by the ship's bow and then electrocuted by lightning. (Ouch!)

VILLAINESS: Miss Trunchbull, *Matilda* (1996)
HOW BAD IS SHE? In the original book by Roald Dahl and in the movie, Miss Trunchbull—the headmistress of Crunchem Hall—is a former Olympic athlete. The hulking tyrant uses her shot-put, javelin, and hammer-throw skills to hurl students over fences and out of classroom windows. For the tiniest offense, she also locks them in "the chokey," a dark closet lined with nails and broken glass. For bigger offenses, she gets cruelly creative. To punish a boy for stealing food, she forces him to eat an enormous chocolate cake in front of the entire school. Trunchbull's motto? "Use the rod, beat the child!"

VILLAINESS: The Other Mother, *Coraline* (2009)
HOW BAD IS SHE? Coraline and her neglectful parents move into a sprawling old house. One rainy day, she finds a locked door that leads to a distorted-mirror version of her own house. There, she meets "Other Mother" and "Other Father." They look just like her parents, except for the big black button eyes sewn to their faces. Coraline enjoys all the attention they give her until…Other Mother tells Coraline that to stay with them, she'll need button eyes sewn into her face, too.

• • •

Q: What happened when the ghost got lost in the fog?
A: He was mist.

RUN, MUMMY, RUN!

· ·

It's a ghoulish race to the finish line!

WHAT YOU NEED: A big pack of toilet-paper rolls (one roll for each player), a bag for recycling paper, designated Start and Finish lines, and teams of two people each.

1. The game begins when the official shouts, "Run, Mummy! Run!"

2. One player on each team stands with arms at sides and feet together, while the other player quickly wraps him from head to toe in toilet paper so he looks exactly like a mummy. (Caution: don't wrap so tightly that the mummy can't hop.)

3. Once wrapped, the mummy must hop all the way to the finish line, cross it, and then return to where he started.

4. That mummy breaks out of the mummy wrap and now wraps his teammate in toilet paper.

5. The second mummy hops to the finish line, turns, and hops back.

6. The first team to have both mummies return home, scoop up all their mummy wrappings, and stuff them into the recycling bag wins.

FINGER FOODS

· · · · · · · · · · · · · · · · · · · ·

These treats will change your view of finger foods forever.

CHEESY FINGERS

WHAT YOU'LL NEED: A bag of your favorite flavor of string cheese, sliced almonds, softened cream cheese, and a butter knife

WHAT TO DO: If wrapped, unwrap each string cheese "finger." Cut each one in half so you end up with two kid-sized "fingers." Use the flat side of a butter knife to press knuckle marks into each finger. Then use a bit of cream cheese to attach a sliced-almond "fingernail" at the tip of each finger. Serve and eat!

BLOODY FINGER BONES

WHAT YOU'LL NEED: Store-bought breadstick dough, marinara sauce, garlic salt, Parmesan cheese, nonstick cooking spray, cookie sheet

WHAT TO DO: Spray the cookie sheet with nonstick spray. Pull apart the breadsticks and space them out on the sheet. Flatten out the ends of each one, then roll up the ends to form "knuckles." Sprinkle each fingerbone with garlic salt and Parmesan cheese, then bake as directed on the package. While they cool, warm the marinara sauce in a microwave. Then dip your finger bones in the marinara "blood" and chow down.

SNAKES IN THE TOILET!

· ·

Heard of snakes on a plane? Well, some New Yorkers are having an even worse problem.

CORN ON THE JOB

Early one morning, a Bronx man shuffled into his bathroom. As he approached the toilet, something moved. He took a step closer and saw a huge white-and-yellow snake with beady red eyes coiled just where he needed to sit. He sprang into action—running out of the bathroom, jumping on top of his kitchen table, and screaming with fear. Then he called 9-1-1. Two minutes later, he called again. The police finally arrived and bagged a corn snake, which is a species of rat snake. Before corn snakes started hanging out in Bronx toilets, they used to hang out in corn silos, waiting to chow down on rats that hung out in the corn. A corn snake is harmless to humans—it might bite your bottom if you sat on it, which would sting a little.

KING IN THE THRONE

Allen Shepard found a different species hissing inside his Staten Island toilet: a brown-and-white-striped California Kingsnake. The snake slithered onto the rim of the toilet and prepared to strike. Shepard called a plumber, grabbed a broom, and beat at the snake, which coiled itself around the broom and held on for dear life. When the plumber arrived and took over the tug-of-war, he had to back all the way out of the bathroom to pull the 4-foot-long Kingsnake out of Shepard's toilet. He tucked the snake into a cooler and took it to the Humane Society. Now, Shepard never goes to the bathroom without checking the toilet, the sink, the bathtub, and then the toilet again. And no one ever has to tell him to put the seat down!

PYTHON IN THE PIPES

Late one night, Nadege Brunacci from Brooklyn found a monstrous python peering up from the depths of her toilet. She slammed down the lid and put a heavy box on it. Then she started calling every agency she could think of to come and get the snake. Many didn't believe her, and the ones who did said, "We don't do snakes." It's no wonder: Pythons strike their prey and then suffocate it in their coils. The bigger a python gets, the more dangerous it is to humans. Finally, the fire department came to Brunacci's rescue. By then, the python had retreated back into the pipes, and plumbers had to tear apart the downstairs neighbor's pipes to capture the enormous (7-foot-long!) reptile. Now, Brunacci looks over her shoulder at the toilet whenever she brushes her teeth. And if she has to go potty in the middle of the night, she uses her daughter's potty-chair rather than risk another late-night encounter with a slithery serpent.

A CHILLIN' TALE

· ·

An Uncle John's Eerily Twisted Tale

I'**VE ALWAYS BEEN** one of those people who knows exactly what she likes. Favorite food: cheesecake. Favorite color: grayish-blue. Favorite pastime? Duh, that's easy. I like to hang out. Preferably in the family room on the burgundy chair. But really, I'm not picky. I have what you'd call a preternatural ability (just learned that word from the Discovery Channel) to get comfortable just about anywhere.

I'm used to getting a lot of flak for doing what I do best. I've even been called lazy. But honestly, I don't see it that way. I mean, if you ask me, I just know how to relax. That's a skill most people don't have. And, really, what's the point of running around like crazy all your life?

If you're going to be as idle as someone like me, there are two important rules: One, don't hesitate to use any object or person to help you get more comfortable. Even a fire hydrant has worked for me in a pinch. And two, don't engage in arguments about your "laziness" with your parents. A solid "WHATEVER" will usually irritate them so much they'll leave you alone.

I'm pretty sure it was breaking rule number two that landed me in trouble. My mom asked why I was too lazy to clean my own room, and I told her I wasn't lazy. I just had a "low energy level." Mom told her Reiki instructor what I'd said, and she recommended that we go to this weird apothecary shop for one of their special teas. The gaunt man behind the counter listened to my mom go on and on about how I never seem to get up from the couch, how I watch too much TV, the usual. Then he pierced me with his bulging black eyes (seriously, they were solid black like an ant's or something), and said, "What is it that *you* want?"

I shrugged. "I just want to chill. Is that so bad?"

The old man blinked, once, twice, and then he started zig-zagging from shelf to shelf grabbing bottles and emptying their contents into a small golden bowl. Dried flowers that smelled musty and sweet. Crumbling pieces of cinnamon-scented bark. A gooey paste that looked like something that had oozed out of an old wound. Finally, he ground the whole mess together with a marble pestle and poured boiling water from a teapot over it.

"A tea to give you exactly what you want," he said, holding out the golden bowl.

I looked at my mom to see if she was serious about this baloney. She just stood there, grinning and looking excited. I decided that if drinking some wacko tea would get me back to my burgundy chair, then it would be worth it. I held my nose (literally) and chugged it down.

When we got to the car, I wasn't sure if I was actually feeling weird or just thinking I felt weird. Of course my mom started asking me over and over again, "How do you feel?" which made the short trip home feel like it took a week. "Tired," is all I told her, which couldn't have been further from the truth. In fact, I'd never felt more energetic. I now knew exactly what it meant to have butterflies in your stomach.

But by the time we pulled into the driveway, the butterflies wanted to burst free. I made a beeline for the chair, clenching my teeth so I wouldn't spew. The velvety fabric felt cool when I collapsed into it, like deep morning earth. I sank down and waited for the butterfly flurry to pass. And finally, it did.

I felt fine now—stiff, but fine. And thirsty. Suddenly, water seemed like the most amazing thing on the planet. For some reason, I kicked off my shoes and wiggled my toes into the carpet. Something wet and full of life-giving energy seeped into my toes, into my legs, and up, up, up through my entire body. *Ahh!* I opened my eyes and looked down at my feet. "MOM!!!!!" My toes hadn't just sunk into the carpet. They'd turned into gnarly roots that went right down through the floor into the earth itself.

My mother came running, then she screamed and rushed for the phone. She dialed a number, then listened, her eyes going wider by the moment. When she hung up, she looked like she was trying to keep from sobbing, being sick, or fainting. "That man. From the store. He-he said, 'I brewed a tea that would give her exactly what she wanted. That is all.'"

And so I sit in the burgundy chair, just chilling… and I'll be sitting here for my entire (tree-long) life.

THE END

NATURE'S BEASTS

· ·

Sure, they have claws that can rip out your throat and venom that can drop you in your tracks. But are nature's scariest creatures really dangerous to humans? You decide.

BEAST: Grizzly bear
SCIENTIFIC NAME: *Ursus arctos horribilis*
LIVES IN: North America

FEAR FACTORS: These bears can be massive, standing up to 8 feet tall and weighing in at 800 pounds or more. They are at the top of nature's food chain and have no problem gobbling down large animals such as moose or bison. And grizzlies can run. They've been clocked at up to 30 mph chasing prey. They have excellent hearing and a killer sense of smell.

THE TRUTH: Grizzlies do feast on other animals, but they mostly eat nuts, berries, leaves, and roots. As for humans? Not so much. Still—like humans—grizzlies are omnivores: they'll eat just about anything, from pine nuts to cutworm moths to fish and "winter kill" carrion: animals that die during the winter. Humans who interfere with a mother bear tending cubs are asking for trouble. Otherwise, grizzlies tend to be shy and will keep their distance—unless you leave food out where their clever grizzly noses can find it.

BEAST: Mexican Redknee Tarantula

SCIENTIFIC NAME: *Brachypelma smithi*

LIVES IN: North America

FEAR FACTORS: These furry spiders have huge needle-sharp fangs and bright red hair on their knees. And they're as big as an adult's hand. They use their bite to kill prey and turn its insides into an slurpy edible liquid.

THE TRUTH: These little creatures are relatively tame towards humans. They mostly eat mice, birds, insects, and other spiders. They can bite, but their venom is very weak and feels a bit like being stung by a bee. In fact, humans pose far more danger to these spiders than they do to us. They're now endangered in the wild because so many people keep them as pets.

BEAST: Black mamba

SCIENTIFIC NAME: *Dendroaspis polylepis*

LIVES IN: Africa

FEAR FACTORS: The black mamba is a massive snake, growing up to 14 feet long. These giant reptiles can slither at up to 12 miles per hour, which makes them the fastest snakes on earth. Watch out! Before they bite, they rear up like a cobra. Their venom is deadly. Those who don't receive antivenom right away can die within 20 minutes.

THE TRUTH: Black mambas are afraid of humans. Instead of using their speed for aggressive behavior, black mambas race to *escape* when they feel threatened. But if provoked, they will bite…multiple times.

BEAST: Gray Wolf

SCIENTIFIC NAME: *Canis lupus*

LIVES IN: North America

FEAR FACTORS: These mammals look like large dogs, but they're much more aggressive and wild. They travel in packs and circle in to attack other large animals such as deer and caribou. A single wolf can eat up to 30 pounds of meat in one sitting. Gray wolves are known for their famously loud howls. Their noses are powerful and they can smell dinner from miles away.

THE TRUTH: Wolves may attack other animals including pets, but they usually stay far away from humans. There has never been a documented case of a wild wolf killing a human in the U.S. Biologists sometimes crawl into wolf dens to look at pups and the adult wolves will just run away.

BEAST: Red-bellied Piranha

SCIENTIFIC NAME: *Pygocentrus nattereri*

LIVES IN: South America

FEAR FACTORS: These fish are best known their deadly, triangle-shaped, razor-sharp teeth. A school of hungry piranha can strip the flesh from the bones of a large mammal—say, a human—in minutes.

THE TRUTH: Despite their terrible reputation in movies and pop culture, piranhas rarely attack humans. In fact, red-bellied piranhas would rather eat fish and water plants than chow down on people. But they won't hestitate to feed on animals that are already dead.

WHO'S AFRAID?

. . . .

To fear or not to fear, that is the real question.

"As a child, I was more afraid of tetanus shots than, for example, Dracula."
—**Dave Barry**

"Don't let the fear of striking out hold you back."
—**Babe Ruth**

"To be honest, I'm scared to death of roller-coaster rides."
—**Liam Neeson**

"Fear makes strangers of people who would be friends."
—**Shirley MacLaine**

"Courage is resistance to fear, mastery of fear, not absence of fear."
—**Mark Twain**

"Love will find a way through paths where wolves fear to prey."
—**Lord Byron**

"I'm the kind of person that when I get up to go use the bathroom, I have this big long hallway, and I just know someone's going to jump out and get me."
—**Britney Spears**

"I have a fear of being boring."
—**Christian Bale**

"A lot of people ask me when I do a stunt, 'Jackie, are you scared?' Of course, I'm scared. I'm not Superman."
—**Jackie Chan**

EXPLODING URINE

· · · · · · · · · · · · · · · · · · · ·

Here's a whiz of an idea!

FOR CENTURIES, some scientists (called alchemists until 1834) were obsessed with the idea of turning cheap metals like lead and iron into gold. They did all kinds of experiments, including this one: In 1669, a German alchemist named Hennig Brand urinated in a tub and let it stand for several days. He then boiled the putrified urine until all that was left was a stinking paste. He heated the paste, hoping that the vapors it emitted would settle into a container of water and condense into...gold. (Really, Hennig?)

It didn't. What remained was a white, waxy substance that glowed in the dark. When Hennig exposed the substance to the air—*Kapowee!*—it exploded into flames! Brand had managed to isolate a previously unknown substance—white phosphorus.

"The discovery of white phosphorus was an important one in early chemistry," wrote Theodore Gray in *Popular Science* magazine. Just mix it with water and you get *phosphoric acid* a chemical now added to skin-care products, anti-nausea medicines, dental cement, fuel cells, and...cola drinks. So, the next time you gulp down a cold Coke or Pepsi, say a big thank you to Hennig Brand's incredible exploding pee!

DON'T BUG ME!

· ·

Here's the buzz on our favorite creepy bug films.

JOE'S APARTMENT (1996)
BUG: Cockroach

PLOT: Joe (Jerry O'Connell) is a guy living in a horrible New York City apartment in a building slated for demolition. The place is filled with hundreds of mischievous, smart-alecky roaches who sing, and even have their own public-access cable TV channel. When Joe finds out an evil property developer wants to tear down his building, the cockroaches "call in favors from every roach, rat, and pigeon in New York City" to try to save the day. No cockroaches were smushed or otherwise harmed in the making of this movie.

THE WASP WOMAN (1959)

BUG: Wasp

PLOT: Janice Starlin (Susan Cabot) is a model who founded her own cosmetics company. Until now, she has always modeled for her company's advertisements. But now that she's in her 40's (talk about old!), investors want her replaced by a younger model. In desperation, she consults a scientist working on a youth serum based on wasp hormones. And she's so desperate to look young, she agrees to be the first human test subject. Bad idea: She's transformed into a murderous queen wasp with huge bulging bug eyes and horrifying mandibles. (No more lipstick commercials for this lady.)

THE FLY (1958)

BUG: Fly

PLOT: Andre Delambre (David Hedison) is a brilliant but eccentric scientist who invents a teleportation device. Sounds like a good idea. If it works, the machine will instantly transfer people and things from one place to another. Bad idea: Delambre tries to transport himself, but a fly gets caught in the chamber with him. Result: their atoms mix together, turning the scientist into a giant man/fly hybrid.

THEM! (1954)

BUG: Giant ants

PLOT: This was the first of the "big bug" flicks. Police Sgt. Ben Peterson (James Whitmore) and his partner find a little girl wandering alone in the New Mexico desert. After they revive her, she screams out one word: "Them!" Them what? Them…ants! Turns out giant ants have been attacking the locals. New Mexico's deserts were home to some of the era's atomic bomb tests. And radiation from those tests caused common ants to mutate into giant man-eating monsters that threaten civilization. To make things worse, two queen ants have flown to Los Angeles to start a new colony beneath the city. (Horrors!)

SKELETON KEYS

. . . .

*Future scientists can use your bones to unlock
the secrets of who you were.*

- **You were male (or female).** Men and women both
  have a pelvis, but the structure differs because women
  give birth. If the pelvis is wide and shallow, the skeleton
  belonged to a female. If it's narrow, it was a male's.
- **You were healthy and wealthy (or not).** Worn teeth
  show a poor diet. Straight, well-maintained teeth show
  good eating habits and enough money for dental care.
- **You were tall (or short).** The longer your forearm and
  leg bones are, the taller you were in life.
- **You worked with your hands (or didn't).** If your
  wrist bones have tiny ridges in them, you probably did
  manual labor for a living. Ridges form where muscles
  attach and pulled against the bone for years.
- **You were right- (or left-) handed.** Muscles become
  stronger and the bones get more worn down at the
  point where they're attached to your bones. If your
  skeleton's right wrist has more wear than the left, you
  were right-handed.
- **You were accident prone.** Cracks and holes in bones
  show childhood injuries. If you broke a bone as a kid,
  your skeleton can still show a tiny fracture many years
  after the break happened.

HARRY POTTY
&
THE CHAMBERPOT
OF SECRETS

....

Eyewitness accounts of ghosts in the bathroom.

GRANDMA'S GOTTA GO!

A woman named Candice shared this story on a
ghost-study website: "One day I was laying in my bed
petting my cat. All of a sudden, something compelled
me to take a picture of my bathroom. I asked my
daughter to grab the camera, and I took a picture of
the bathroom. When I looked at the photo, I saw
a face right beside the toilet! It looks a lot like my
grandmother who died a few years ago."

THE LITTLE MER-GHOST

A mom and her son had dinner at a Little Mermaid
theme restaurant called Ariel's Grotto in Disney
California Adventure Park. Here's their story: "We
finished our meal, and my son ran off to use the restroom.
The next thing I know, he comes running out. He told
me, 'I was in there alone, when suddenly a few toilets
started flushing, then I heard stall doors opening and

closing! I looked out of the door and saw that no one was in the bathroom!' He was totally freaked out. I tried to tell him that maybe someone came in and ran out, but he was completely insistent that no one came in!"

A POO-LITE SPIRIT

This bathroom ghost reminds us of Moaning Myrtle from the Harry Potter books...only much nicer. Here's the story, shared by a grade school student named Jenny: "I remember one time at school, a janitor told me not to enter the bathroom on the third floor. It was rumored to be haunted. One day, I needed to use the toilet very urgently, so I asked my teacher for permission. I rushed to the nearest one. It was the one the janitor had warned me about. I went in, and no one else was in there. I sat down, and then I heard the sound of a little girl's voice. She said, 'Hello. Nice to meet you.' She added, 'Welcome to my toilet,' and 'Let's play again tomorrow.' I ran away as fast as I could and never used that bathroom again!"

THAT SINKING FEELING

A man named Steve D. shared this tale on About.com's "Paranormal Phenomena" page: "A few years ago in South Yorkshire, England, I was woken up by the sound of water dripping in my bathroom. As I got up to turn it off, the light in the bathroom wouldn't turn on, which was very daunting at the time. Nevertheless, I attempted to turn the tap off anyway, when a picture on the wall suddenly fell and landed in the sink. I ran back into my room! The next day, the light worked fine. To this day, I rarely venture into my bathroom at night."

I SEE YOU!

A ghost hunter whose screen name is "EVP Researcher" specializes in finding EVPs. Short for "Electronic Voice Phenomena," EVPs are recordings of ghostly voices. "On October, 18, 2008, I was investigating County Home and Lunatic House in Ohio. Way out back, there were two Port-A-Potties set up in the pitch dark. I went in and was going #1. All of a sudden, and very loudly, I heard a voice say, 'I seeee you.' It sounded like a snake. I laughed and said, 'I hope not!' I finished up and stepped outside. Nobody was around! I pulled my digital audio recorder out of my pocket and started recording. I said, 'Say it again.' The ghost said it again: 'I see you.' And then it said, 'I talked to you earlier.' I still don't know why the ghost was peeking at people in the Port-A-Potties."

• • •

THE EVIL EYE

All over Greece people wear dark blue glass charms with eyes at their center. Taxi drivers dangle them from rear-view mirrors. Girls wear them on necklaces. People even hang them on their front doors. According to locals, blue glass eyes provide protection against "the evil eye"—a curse caused by envy or admiration. It's a bit tricky: Someone can "eye" you without even meaning to. (Hey! Nice hair! Oops…) Some Greeks blame the evil eye for headaches, upset stomachs, or even unexplained deaths.

THE VULTURE

....

An Uncle John's Totally Twisted Tale

Once upon an evening cloudy,
as I blasted music loudly
Over a quaint and boring schoolbook
that had made me start to snore...
From my window came a-tapping—
echoing, persistent flapping.
Was it just the music rapping...
rapping louder than the score?
"Open up!" a grim voice uttered.
"My claws are getting very sore."
Only this, then nothing more.

When I saw what there awaited;
well, I very nearly fainted.
Great and hulking was the creature
hunched upon the sill—and reeking.
Said he, "I'm no cute canary.
That's the burden that I carry—
but truly, I am not that scary.
Please, don't fear me anymore!"
Then the raw, repulsive creature
swept in like my phys. ed. teacher,
Stood upon my homework drooling—
drooling on my bedroom floor.

Once inside, he licked his chops.
"Now that's enough!" I shrieked. "Please stop."
"I must be fed." The vile one said.
It lunged. I dove beneath the bed.
"Come out...come out. You need not fear."
It bit me then—right on the rear.
Its mouth gaped wide, and in I threw
socks and sneakers, Fido, too.
Plastic soldiers, a ball (or four),
jacks and marbles, an apple core...
At last, the vulture cried, "No more!"

"What have you done?" The dread bird moaned.
And from its gut there came a groan.
A bellow, a rumble, a belch did start.
It clutched its belly and ripped...a fart.
The stench that swept across my room
filled me with horror. I gagged. I swooned.
I quaked and trembled 'neath my bed.
It hopped to the window and turned its head.
The fiend, that nasty carnivore,
its yellow eyes my own implored.
Then quoth the vulture—"Nevermore!"

THE END

"Airplanes are a good place to write poetry and then firmly throw it away. My collected works are mostly on the vomit bags of Pan Am and TWA." —**Charles McCabe**

UNLUCKY 13

. . . .

This number has a seriously bad reputation.

- In Norse myth, a hero named Balder was killed at a banquet by the mischievous god Loki. Loki had crashed a party of 12, becoming the 13th person.
- In ancient Rome, witches met in groups of 12. They left the 13th spot open for the devil.
- In 1307, on Friday the 13th King Philip of France tortured the Knights Templar.
- No airport in Scotland has a gate 13, instead they have gate 12B.
- "Houston, we've had a problem." Those historic words were spoken by Apollo 13 command module pilot Jack Swigert. The problem: an oxygen tank had exploded aboard the spacecraft. The date: April 13, 1970.
- More than 80 percent of high-rise buildings don't have a 13th floor. Most skip right to floor 14.
- In Formula One racing, there is no car with the number 13.
- President Franklin D. Roosevelt never invited 13 guests to lunch. If someone canceled and it looked as if there might be 13 people at the table, he invited his secretary to join the group.
- Universal Studios has no studio 13.
- Fear of the number 13 has a name: *triskaidekaphobia.*

Through the Forest in the Night

by Valeri Gorbachev

One day Frankenstein, Mummy, and Witch were driving through the forest.

IN THE NEWS: DEAD THIRSTY

. . . .

Once again, truth really is stranger than fiction.

REMEMBER WHEN YOU WERE LITTLE, and woke up from a deep sleep with a big thirst? That's what happened to two-year-old Kelvin Santos in 2012. What made such an ordinary event newsworthy? The day before, Kelvin had been pronounced dead by his doctors in a hospital in Belem, Brazil.

Little Kelvin had been suffering from pneumonia and had stopped breathing. After his death, his grieving parents took him home. Family members held an all-night wake, gathering around the little boy's coffin. An hour before his funeral was to take place, Kelvin sat up in his coffin. "Daddy, can I have some water?" he asked.

According to his father, Antonio Santos, everyone started to scream. They thought a miracle had taken place. "Then Kelvin just lay back down," said Santos. "We couldn't wake him. He was dead again."

Santos rushed his son back to the hospital, but doctors confirmed that he showed no signs of life. The family delayed the funeral once more, hoping Kelvin would wake again, but his thirst for life seemed to be quenched. Kelvin was laid to rest in the local cemetery.

TOO ICKY TO EAT

. . . .

*Those weird-sounding ingredients on food labels
may be creepier than you think!*

CASTOREUM. The bad news: This food flavoring is
from the castor sac scent glands of male and female
beavers. These glands are (unfortunately) located at
the butt end of the beaver. The even badder news: You
probably can't avoid eating the stuff. It's usually listed on
the label as "natural flavoring."

CARMINE. Most people freak when an insect lands
on their food. But what if insects are part of the recipe?
Guess what? They are. Carmine is a red food coloring
that comes from boiled cochineal bugs—a type of beetle.
Because it can cause allergic reactions in some people, if
carmine is in a food, it must be clearly listed on a label.
By the way, carmine can be found in Good n' Plenty, ice
cream, lemonade, and grapefruit juice.

SHELLAC. This is the stuff that makes jelly beans,
candy corn, and other hard-coated candies look shiny. (It
might be listed as "confectioners glaze" on the label.) This
ingredient also comes to us from the insect kingdom.
Shellac is the sticky substance made from the secretions
of the female Kerria lacca, an insect found in Thailand.

SILICON DIOXIDE. This substance can be found on every beach. It gets in your bathing suit, your hair, and shoes. Yep: silicon dioxide is sand. And, believe it or not, sand can be found in salt, soup, shredded cheese, and coffee creamer. It absorbs moisture and helps keep the rest of the ingredients from clumping.

VIRUSES. Mom probably never told you to eat your viruses, but if she slapped a slice of bologna on your sandwich, she should have! *Bacteriophages*—tiny bacteria-killing viruses—can actually kill off a dangerous bacteria called *listeria*. Listeria causes fever, a stiff neck, confusion, weakness, vomiting, and sometimes diarrhea. Manufacturers spray bacteriophages on ready-to-eat deli meats and hot dogs to keep listeria from growing on these prepared meats. Check the ingredient list for "bacteriophage preparation."

• • •

30 MINUTES

Video game characters aren't the only ones who can gain or lose time on their "lives." According to a statistics professor at Cambridge University, people can, too.

Add 30 minutes
- Exercise for 10 minutes
- Eat 1.25 servings of fruit
- Eat 1.25 servings of veggies
- Drink 2 cups of coffee a day

Subtract 30 minutes
- Smoke 2 cigarettes
- Watch 2 hours of TV without moving
- Eat a hamburger

SPOOKIFIED PINS

. . . .

Looking for a ghoulish accessory? Look no further!

WHAT YOU NEED:

- Discarded magazines
- Clean plastic lids (like those on yogurt or sour cream containers)
- Construction paper in creepy colors, such as black, orange, and slime green (Include a color that's easy to write on, such as yellow.)

- Scissors
- Glitter glue
- Craft glue
- Glue stick
- Fine-tip markers
- Poster board
- Self-adhesive pin backs (available at craft stores)

WHAT TO DO:

1. Leaf through the magazines and cut out pictures to "spookify." For example, a photo of a cute kitten can become downright scary when you add blood-red-tipped teeth and a construction-paper witch's hat. And lovely models turn creepy when you give them "stitched" foreheads and Frankenstein neck bolts.

2. Choose a lid for the base of your pin. Trace around the lid onto the construction paper of your choice, cut out the circle, and use the glue stick to attach it to the top of your lid.

3. Glue-stick your spookified picture to the construction-paper-covered lid. Sparkle it up with glitter glue for a ghostly glow effect (if desired).

4. Next, come up with a scary-funny caption for your pin. Think of what your pin character might say. ("Happy Halloween!" or "Boo!" work, but they've been…uhm…done to death.) So go for something clever and original. Here are a few idea starters:

- Bat's all folks! (bat)
- Bite me! (vampire)
- #1 Speller (witch)
- Trick or treat…or else! (monster)
- Rest in Pieces! (zombie)

5. After you've created your caption, use a black fine-tip marker to write it (pin-size) on yellow construction paper, and draw a speech bubble around it. Craft-glue the speech bubble onto poster board to make it sturdy. Wait till the glue dries, and then cut it out. Now craft-glue the speech bubble onto your pin so it looks like your character is talking.

6. To finish, peel the paper off the self-adhesive pin back, and stick the pin back inside the plastic lid. Don't stop now! Spookify pins for all your friends.

• • •

FEAR FACTOR: The Summum company of Salt Lake City mummifies human bodies. Cost? $67,000.

BRAVE HEARTS

. . . .

When danger strikes, most people freeze or run.
Not these kids. They turned into superheroes.

HERO: 11-year-old Prasannata Shandilya, India
THE HEROIC DEED: Stopping a home invasion
WHAT HAPPENED: One evening in 2011, Prasannata
was in her room near the kitchen when she heard her
parents screaming. Robbers had invaded their house.
They were demanding the family's valuables and brutally
beating her parents. Prasannata knew she had to do
something. "I tiptoed into the kitchen," she said, "and
prepared a mix of turmeric and chili powder." Then she
slipped into the room with the robbers and threw the
spicy mix into their eyes. The robbers fled, eyes streaming.
"She has always been a smart kid," said her father. "We
were amazed by her courage and are proud of her."

HERO: 11-year-old Jonah Yano, Hawaii
HEROIC DEED: Thwarting a car thief
WHAT HAPPENED: Jonah and his 9-year-old sister were
sitting in their dad's pickup truck in front of their house.
Seconds earlier, Mr. Yano had walked to the back of
the truck to grab something. He noticed a man walking
across the street toward the truck, but before he could
react, the man jumped into the driver's seat and took off

down the road with the kids. What the car-jacker didn't know: Jonah is a student of Brazilian jiu-jitsu. "I grabbed his shoulder and started punching his face, telling him to get out of the truck," Jonah told reporters. Jonah's fast fists gave his dad time to catch up with the truck and pull the criminal out of it. Jonah said he wasn't scared, even though the thief was much bigger than he was. All he could think about was protecting his sister.

HERO: 15-year-old Mohamed Ibrahim, the Maldives
HEROIC DEED: Stopping an assassination
WHAT HAPPENED: In 2008, President Maumoon Abdul Gayoom of the Maldives—an island nation in the Indian Ocean—stood before a cheering crowd. Nearby, dressed for the occasion in his blue Boy Scout uniform, Mohamed waited in line to greet the president. Suddenly, a man rushed at the president with a knife. Mohamed reacted instantly. He grabbed the knife with his bare hands, deflecting it enough that all it did was rip the president's shirt. "There was blood on the president's shirt," said Gayoom's spokesman. "But it was the boy's." Though Mohamed's hand needed stitches, his bravery was applauded. How'd he know what to do? His training as a Boy Scout taught him to "Be Prepared."

HERO: 10-year-old Priyanshu Joshi, India
HEROIC DEED: Saving his sister from a leopard
WHAT HAPPENED: Priyanshu and his sister were walking to school one day when a leopard sprang at the

girl. Within moments, the big cat had torn loose her earlobe. "There was no time to waste," said Priyanshu. "My school bag became my weapon. I began hitting him with the bag. I also punched him." Luckily, a noisy army vehicle passed by and distracted the leopard. "Otherwise, it would have carried us away," said Priyanshu. In 2010, the Indian Prime Minister gave the bag-toting leopard fighter a National Bravery Award.

HERO: 8-year-old Reese Ronceray, New Jersey
HEROIC DEED: Saved a kid from drowning
WHAT HAPPENED: Reese was playing near a lake with his 5-year-old neighbor. When the younger boy fell into deep water, Reese remembered an episode of *SpongeBob SquarePants* in which one character rescues another who is drowning. Reese jumped right in after his friend. He tucked the younger boy under one arm and paddled with the other—the same technique he saw on *SpongeBob*. "We just plopped and went under the water," Reese said, "but I kept moving my arms all the way to the surface." Reese paddled his young neighbor to safety. What did the boy's mom say to her son's rescuer? "Thank you. Thank you. Thank you. Thank you," Reese told an interviewer. (Who says cartoons have no redeeming value?)

●   ●   ●

TONGUE TWISTED
Sixteen skeletons juggle skulls by the seashore.

GRUESOME GREECE

· ·

As they say in Greece: "May the earth not eat you!"

I DIG GREECE

The Greek Orthodox cemetery in Steni on the island of Evvia—an hour east of Athens—looks perfectly ordinary at first. It has classic white marble graves with crosses, decorated with faded portraits of the deceased. What is extraordinary? The open graves: six in all. One open grave has a red bucket sticking out of freshly-dug dirt piled beside it. Another contains a coffin that has been broken open. What's the story here? Grave robbers? Escape of the undead? Not exactly.

When author John Mole and his family moved to a Greek village in the 1970s, he spotted open graves similar to those in Steni. He, too, wondered what was going on in Greek cemeteries. Mole found his answer when a neighbor invited him to her Uncle Christos's… exhumation. That's right. Three to ten years after an official burial, Greek families dig up the remains of their loved ones. This practice takes place all over Greece.

THE HOUSE OF BONES

"The worst part was not knowing what condition old Christos was going to be in," writes Mole in his book, *It's All Greek to Me*. Mole watched his host's wife, Elipda, dig up the skull, inspect it, and brush off the "brown scabby bits" he hoped were just dirt. Then she kissed the top of the skull and passed it up to another family member. As the skull made the rounds, Elipda kept digging until the grave was empty. Meanwhile, a half-dozen women scrubbed and dried every bone from Uncle Christos's body and packed them all into a box. Finally, everyone— Mole included—headed to a small building that looked like a storage shed. It was, in fact, the community *osteofilakio*, or bone house. The bone house would be Uncle Christos's final resting place.

Here's the thing: Greece is about the size of Alabama. For a country, that's not very big. So burial space is at a premium. Add the fact that the Greek Orthodox Church bans cremation, and you get…family members digging up the dead. If the graves weren't emptied to make room for new arrivals, Greece could turn into one giant cemetery.

DEAD YUMMY

Greeks believe that spirits stick around after the funeral, so families hold regular gravesite parties. The first happens nine days after the funeral. The next: 40 days after the funeral. The celebrations go on and on until the dead— or what's left of them—are dug up and moved to the bone house.

For these and other gravesite occasions, Greeks have special food for the dead called *kollyva*. They bake sweet cakes decorated with the words *Kalo Taxidi* ("Have a good journey!"). And they hand out little bags filled with a mixture of grains, seeds, nuts, and dried fruit. Families lug trays of the stuff to cemeteries on special days for the dead such as "Soul Saturday."

One widow put it this way: "When you see someone in your dreams, it's the soul you see. People in your dreams eat, don't they? The souls of the dead eat, too."

IT'S GREEK TO US, TOO!

- The word *cemetery* comes from the Greek word for sleeping place, *koimeterion*.
- *Necrophobia* means an extreme fear of death or dead bodies and comes from the Greek words *nekros* (corpse) and *phobos* (fear).
- An *osteopath* is a doctor who treats illnesses by manipulating the bones. The word comes from the Greek *osteon*—bone.
- Homer's ancient epic poem *The Odyssey* follows the journey of the Greek hero Odysseus. In the eleventh book, Odysseus travels to Hades (the underworld) hoping to find a way home. Greeks call this book *nekyia*. The word comes from the Greek word for dead: *necro*.
- The grim-reaper figure associated with death was likely based on the Greek god Chronos. In Greek myth, Chronos was the god of the harvest (which is why he carries that creepy scythe) and of time (he's also called Father Time). As the peasant reaps the harvest, so Father Time reaps the souls of humans—when their time comes to an end.

COSTUMED KOOKS

· ·

When kids wear costumes, it's a fun kind of scary. When grownups wear costumes? It's a whole nuther kind of scary.

NIGHT OF THE DRIVING DEAD

When police arrived on the scene of a car accident in Portland, Oregon, in 2010, they couldn't believe their eyes. The five people in the smashed car were all bleeding. Their clothes were torn and splattered with blood and guts. Their skin was white as death. Police feared the worst, until…the five people stumbled out of the car. That's when officers found themselves face-to-face with…*zombies?* Nope, just Portlanders dressed like zombies. They'd been on their way to a costume party when the driver lost control of the car and wrecked. "We're glad that everyone is alive, despite being undead," one officer joked.

GUMBY GONE BAD

Ever heard of Gumby? He's a bendy green clay character who starred in a cartoon Uncle John used to watch as a kid. Gumby still pops up occasionally—like at a 7-Eleven store in San Diego, California, one night in 2011. This was not the good-guy Gumby of kids' cartoons. This was a robber wearing a Gumby costume. When Gumby walked up to the counter and demanded all the money in the register, the clerk thought it was a joke. "I don't have time for this," he said. "I'm cleaning." Then...Gumby reached inside his costume. Was he reaching for a gun? Maybe, but what ended up in Gumby's hand was just loose change. Frustrated, Gumby turned and ran out of the store...leaving his 27¢ behind on the floor.

ATTACK OF THE COW LADY!

An Ohio woman decided that she really wanted to scare people one day. (And, no, it was not Halloween.) She put on a full-body cow costume and walked to a busy sidewalk in her town. Then the "cow lady" started jumping around and yelling and chasing kids who walked too close to her. She even went into the street and blocked traffic. Concerned citizens called the police. When police arrived, the cow lady started yelling at them, too. That's when police made what may have been the first cow arrest in Ohio history. The cow-lady was sentenced to one month in jail.

MOVIE MOM-STER

In 2012, Angelina Jolie was starring in *Maleficent*, a film that tells the Sleeping Beauty tale from the evil queen's point of view. Jolie stayed "in character" during much of the film shoot, even wearing her costume at home. According to the *National Enquirer*, Jolie's six children were "horrified" by their mother's "hideous makeup and huge horns." Her son Knox, age four at the time, ran from "Maleficent Mom."

GHASTLY HEADLINES

....

Real headlines from real newspapers. (Really?)

**Diana Was Still Alive
Hours Before
She Died**

Authorities Pursue Man
Running With Scissors

**GENERAL WHO RAN
SOUTH VIETNAM
BRIEFLY DIES AT 86**

POLICE ARREST
EVERYONE ON
FEBRUARY 22ND

**HOMICIDE VICTIMS
RARELY TALK TO
POLICE**

City Plans Its First Dog
Park, Archery Range

BEHEADING CAN
CAUSE KIDS STRESS

*17 REMAIN DEAD
IN MORGUE
SHOOTING SPREE*

**WOMAN FALLS IN
HOSPITAL
TOLD TO CALL
AMBULANCE**

CITY UNSURE
WHY THE SEWER
SMELLS

Blazing Butt Blamed
for Pine Street Fire

**POLICE SHOOT MAN
WHO WAS STABBING
HIMSELF**

*SEWAGE SPILL KILLS FISH
BUT WATER SAFE TO DRINK*

THE LEGEND OF PEE-PEE HOLLOW

....

An Uncle John's Eerily Twisted Tale!

IKE CRANE DIDN'T MIND crossing the forest to get home in daylight, but it spooked him at night. That's why he always hurried home as soon as school got out, instead of stopping to talk to Katy Van Tassel—the girl of his dreams.

One day, the drama teacher posted a flyer: *Cinderella*, Casting Call next Monday. Kids buzzed around the flyer, speculating on who would win each role. "Katy will be Cinderella," one girl pouted. The girl was right. Katy had played the princess role in every play the school had produced. "That means Brom will be Prince Charming."

Ike's saucer-shaped ears perked up. Prince Charming? He swallowed, and his Adam's apple bobbed up and down his spindly neck. The boy who played Prince Charming would get to kiss Cinderella in the final scene. And if Katy was going to be cast in that role, he'd be trying out.

There were only two problems: one, play practice lasted for three hours after school. Since it was late fall, he'd have to walk home every evening in the dark. Two, the beefy Brom Brunt—who also had a crush on Katy—

would definitely try out for the lead role. Then there was problem number three. (I know. I said two problems. But the third problem is just so embarrassing.)

Here it is: Ike had an unusually small bladder, so he had to urinate frequently. Every day on his walk through the woods, he stopped in a hollow full of hemlock trees to pee. And the more scared he was, the more he needed to go. So how on earth would he make it through an entire three-act play?

Just then, Brom Brunt strutted over and scribbled his name on the sign-up sheet. Ike squared his thin shoulders. No way was he letting that oaf kiss Katy, so as Brom stepped aside, Ike added his name.

"Prince Charming?" Brom snorted. "A walking scarecrow like you? Don't be ridiculous."

Katy pushed past Brom to add her own name to the list. "No more ridiculous than a guy with the charm of a warthog trying out for the role."

When the parts were posted, Ike could not believe his luck. He'd won the role of Prince Charming. Brom stewed in the front row during every rehearsal. That didn't stop Ike from hoping every day that they'd practice the kiss at the end of the last act. They didn't, until the last practice before the play. "OK, you two." The director nodded at Katy, then Ike. "Time for the big moment."

"We don't really have to kiss, do we?" Katy asked.

The director raised his eyebrows. "Uhm...yes? But perhaps we should save the real thing for opening night."

Ike was disappointed. Did Katy not want to kiss

him? He leaned toward her, and they air-kissed with their lips a couple of inches apart. Even that was enough to make Brom Brunt, watching from the front row, seethe with rage.

"Perfect," said the director. "We're all ready for the performance."

As Ike left the auditorium, he overheard Brom mutter, "I'll teach that scarecrow a lesson that will make him stay away from Katy forever."

Ike hurried toward the woods, glancing over his shoulder to make sure Brom hadn't followed him. The full moon cast long shadows that seemed to slither between the trees. Ike walked faster. As he crossed the footbridge over the creek, he heard something that could have been twigs snapping beneath boots or skeletal bones rattling or maybe just branches rubbing together in the wind.

A hair-raising "Hoo-oo-oo" echoed through the woods. It could have been an owl, but the cry sounded eerily human. Ike seriously needed to pee, but he was too afraid to stop before he reached his usual spot. So he gritted his teeth and scurried on.

That's when he saw it—a swirling white mass about twenty feet to his right. Ike's mouth went dry with fear. Wide-eyed and trembling, he broke into a trot. The ghost let out a horrible laugh and kept pace. Ike stretched out his long legs and ran for it. He stumbled over roots and rocks. Low-lying branches slashed his face, but he didn't slow down. He could hear the ghost a few steps behind him and getting closer by the minute.

A desperate (and rather embarrassing) escape plan flashed in his adrenalin-washed brain. He hopped over a fallen log and sprinted into the hemlock hollow, dashing straight for the slippery spot where he peed every day. At the last second, he leaped over the wet spot. The ghost— cold on his heels—did not. Ike heard feet slipping and sliding, then a thud followed by a strangled cry that told him that his pursuer had hit hard.

"Help!" called a pain-wracked voice. "Please! Help me!" Then he heard sniffs and a disgusted voice saying, "What the heck is that smell?"

Ike felt like running all the way home and slamming the door shut behind him. Then he asked himself what Prince Charming would do.

The next night, Ike and Katy peered through the curtains at the packed auditorium. Brom Brunt sat in the front row, crutches by his side, with his leg in a brand-new cast. In just a few minutes, the play would begin. Katy let the curtain fall shut. She turned to Ike. "I was wondering," she said, "if maybe we should practice a bit."

"We've been practicing for two weeks," Ike said. "I think we're ready."

Katy leaned forward. When her face was inches from Ike's, she said, "But we never practiced this." And she kissed him squarely on the lips.

(HOPEFULLY NOT) THE END

SAME MOLD, SAME MOLD

. . . .

*Your parents probably told you not to play with your food,
but did they say not to do science experiments with it?
We didn't think so.*

WHAT YOU NEED:
- Slice of bread
- Cheese
- Fruit, such as apples or oranges
- 2 zip-top plastic bags
- Water
- Masking tape
- Sharpie type marker

WHAT TO DO:

1. Use the marker to write "DRY FOOD" on one bag. Write "WET FOOD" on the other bag.

2. Tear or cut two 1-inch squares from the slice of bread, piece of cheese, and piece of fruit.

3. Put one piece of each in the DRY FOOD bag.

4. Dip the remaining pieces in water and put them in the WET FOOD bag. Keep the bag unsealed for about an hour, and then seal it.

5. Leave both bags in a place where they won't get much light and won't be disturbed.

6. Mold is slow and sneaky, so check the foods daily. It may take a week or two to see the seriously scary stuff. Look as closely as you can, but don't open the bags (see warning on the next page). Which foods grew mold? Did wackier mold come from the wet or dry foods? Do all the molds look the same?

Warning: When you're done, throw away the bags *without opening them*. Breathing in mold can make you sick.

DR. JOHNENSTEIN SAYS: Molds are microscopic fungi. Under the right conditions, they grow into colonies that can be seen without a microscope. The best condition for growing super-scary mold? Warm, damp, and humid (like the inside of a plastic zip-top bag filled with wet food).

A FEW MOLDY FACTS

- No one knows how many mold species exist, but there may be as many as 300,000 kinds.

- You can't get away from molds: They're in the air you breathe and are found both indoors and outdoors.

- Molds produce tiny "spores" that spread through the air like seeds. Lucky spores land in a perfect place to grow (like inside your nose—so don't open the bags!).

- Molds can be any color, including white, orange, green, and black.

- Lots of mold grew in New Orleans after Hurricane Katrina hit in August 2005. After opening up one building, workers saw something "beautiful" on the ceiling: rings within rings in different colors of yellow and gray. What were they? Mold colonies.

- Molds are even tough enough to survive in the Antarctic. They feed on any organic material they can find, including moss and penguin carcasses.

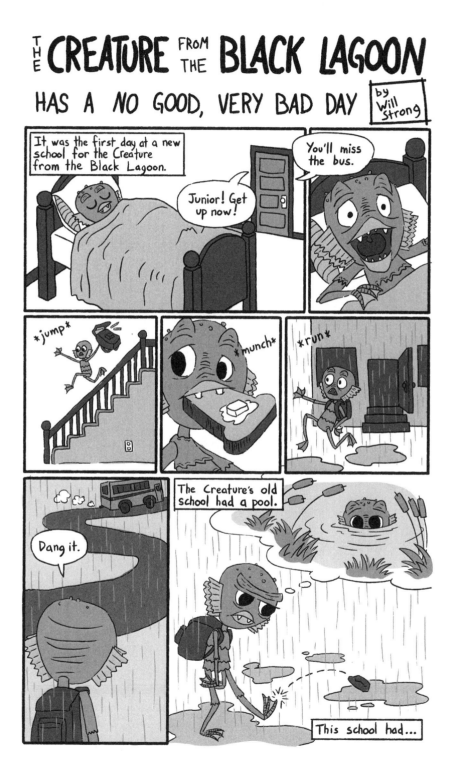

TERRIBLE TYRANTS

· · · · · · · · · · · · · · · · · · · ·

Who put the "rot" in rotten? These guys.

T**YRANT:** Emperor Nero, "The Beast"
WHERE AND WHEN: Rome (A.D. 37–68)
THE TERRIBLE DEEDS: Historians say that Nero dressed people in animal skins and had them attacked by wolves. He boiled villagers in oil. He made people into human candles to light his gardens. In A.D. 64, fire swept through the city of Rome. Some say Nero "fiddled while Rome burned," but since the fiddle had not yet been invented, writers who used that phrase probably meant "fiddled around." In other words, Nero did something frivolous instead of something helpful. One Roman historian said Nero set the fire himself to get rid of "ugly buildings." Probably not. But he did manage to blame the Christians for the fire, and then had thousands of them fed to the lions as punishment.

WHY DID HE DO IT? Many believe Nero was insane. His mother set his bloody reign in motion by murdering her uncle to make her 16-year-old son emperor.

THE TYRANT'S DOWNFALL: After Rome burned, the people of Rome had finally had enough. Nero was removed by the Senators and declared a public enemy, doomed to die. When soldiers came for the tyrant, he stabbed himself in the neck. He seemed to have fiddled about with his own suicide, as his servant had to push him onto his sword to finish the job.

TYRANT: Attila the Hun, "The Scourge of God"
WHERE AND WHEN: Central Asia (A.D. 406–453)
THE TERRIBLE DEEDS: Attila was so short he was almost dwarfish, but that didn't slow him down. He did most of his killing on horseback, like his warrior ancestors. He and his horde of Huns would gallop into a town and cut down anyone in their path. They'd murder men, women, and children; steal what they wanted; and then ride on to the next town or country. Even his wives were cruel. It's said one of them murdered and cooked two of his sons from a different wife and served them to him for dinner. Parts of the Great Wall of China were built to stop Attila, and Hungary bears this warrior's name.
WHY DID HE DO IT? Because a Hun's gotta do what a Hun's gotta do. He came from nomadic people who lived by stealing from other villages. He just happened to do it on a bigger and better scale.
HIS DOWNFALL: The night he married his seventh wife, he went to bed drunk. During the night he got a nosebleed and choked to death on his own blood.

TYRANT: Tamerlane, "Conqueror of the World"
WHERE AND WHEN: Asia (A.D. 1336–1405)
THE TERRIBLE DEEDS: Tamerlane was like a steamroller rumbling across Central Asia, Turkey, and India, destroying everything and everyone in his path.

His enemies were tortured, buried alive, cemented into walls, sliced in half at the waist, beheaded, and hung. He left behind pyramids made of townspeople's skulls: 90,000 skulls in Baghdad alone. He liked to call himself "The Sword of Islam." Scholars estimate that Tamerlane and his army murdered more than 17 million people— 5 percent of the world's population.

WHY DID HE DO IT? He wanted to restore the power others had taken from his people, the Mongols. Though he walked with a limp and was unable to use his right arm, Tamerlane ("Timur the Lame") also wanted to rule the world. He almost succeeded. The more outrageously he behaved in one city—by cruelly butchering every inhabitant—the more likely the next city would surrender without a fight.

HIS DOWNFALL: Tamerlane was on his way to conquer the Chinese Empire when winter hit and he died of a cold.

Want to meet more terrible tyrants? *Turn to page 210.*

• • •

FEAR FACTOR: "Black widow" is a slang term for women who murder their husbands for money. Betty Lou Beets of Gun Barrel City, Texas, killed at least three of her five husbands and buried them in the yard outside her mobile home. Motive: pensions and life insurance money.

FEED THE ANIMALS

· ·

Q: *What happens when you give Halloween pumpkins to zoo animals?* A: *They get gourd!*

THERE'S A NEW HALLOWEEN TREND at zoos in the U.S. and around the world. Seems they've started offering pumpkins to zoo animals as Halloween treats. "They love them," said Tony Franceschiello, Senior Keeper at the San Diego Zoo Safari Park. Most zoo animals have never seen a pumpkin, so they're drawn to the bright orange squash.

Some animals—such as elephants—know exactly what to do pumpkins. "Elephants pretty much crush them," said Franceschiello. "They're melon eaters anyway." A hippo at Chicago's Brookfield Zoo tried to devour her pumpkin, but her huge tusks got in the way. A cheetah cub at the Whipsnade Zoo in England had better luck: it bit the pumpkin's eye out. (Yum!)

Other animals need more encouragement. San Diego zoo keepers put yummy surprises inside for the meerkats. "We spice them up with meal worms," said Franceschiello. Pumpkins for the bat-eared foxes are stuffed with live mice and crickets. Red river hogs like their pumpkins scary. "We put different faces on the pumpkins so they look scared or mad or something," Franceschiello said. "The hogs attack them!"

BANISH TROUBLE

. . . .

*Homework? Zits? Cockroaches? Our sources say this
amazing spell will get rid of things you don't want.*

WHAT YOU NEED:

- 1 apple
- 2 or 3 mint leaves
- 1 skewer
- 1 ribbon

WHAT TO DO:

1. Cut the apple in half to reveal the star at its center. Rub one half of the apple with mint leaves and repeat, "Go away [fill in what you want to banish here]."

2. Use the skewer to carefully rejoin the two halves of the apple.

3. Tie the ribbon around the apple and skewer.

4. Bury the apple in backyard.

WHAT WILL HAPPEN: Our source claims that as the apple rots, whatever has been troubling you will disappear.

• • •

THE BODY FARM

....

If you can read this article without blowing chunks, crime-scene investigation might be the career for you!

SCHOOL OF THE DEAD

Imagine a three-acre forest littered with bodies—some in black plastic bags, some in cardboard boxes, some hidden in car trunks, and others simply lying on their backs with frozen eyes staring skyward. The whole place is surrounded by a razor-wire fence, not to keep the dead in, but to keep the living out. Creepy? Sure. Real? You bet! It's the Anthropological Research Facility (ARF) of the University of Tennessee. It was nicknamed "The Body Farm" by the FBI, and it's for students who study how the body decays.

Corpses have a lot to teach students: from the obvious—race, gender, and age—to the hidden—when and how a person died. It's the kind of information police detectives and FBI agents need to solve murders. Each year about 45 corpses make ARF their final resting place, all in the name of *forensic anthropology*: the science of examining human remains to solve mysteries.

WORKING STIFFS

Exactly what happens to the body when a person dies? First, it begins to stiffen—that's called *rigor mortis*. The stiffening lasts for the first 48 hours after death. The body also begins to cool, which is known as *algor mortis*. The body's temperature drops about 1 degree Fahrenheit every hour after death until it matches the temperature around it. After three days, the body turns from green to purple to black. And then it starts to rot. Once that happens, crime-scene investigators look for other clues to how long the corpse has been dead. They start with...bugs.

STOP BUGGING ME!

Bugs help bodies decompose. As the body rots, bugs show up in a specific order, called *insect succession*. First, blowflies buzz in and start to eat the corpse's body fat. Next, flesh flies arrive and lay eggs. When the eggs hatch, they become maggots. The maggots carry with them bacteria that settle in the abdomen, lungs, and skin of the corpse. Then beetles show up. They lay eggs, too. Other insects scurry over to feed on maggots and beetle larvae. By checking which bugs are on (or in) a body, scientists can tell just how long it has been there.

THE BODY BOUQUET

Dr. William Bass—who founded ARF in 1971—said that the body emits 450 chemicals as it decays. And each stage of decay has a unique smell. Bass has given the stages names, such as *putrescine* and *cadaverine*. Being able to sniff out the stage is important: It helps investigators pinpoint the time of death. With 45 bodies rotting, the stench at the body farm can get pretty strong.

(Locals call the place "BARF.") So how do investigators sniff out a single chemical? With a handheld electronic "nose" invented by an ARF student. The device uses aroma-scan technology developed for the food and wine industry and can sniff out the time of death by identifying the chemicals in a corpse.

SKULL AND BONES

It takes about a month for chemicals and bugs to liquefy a body. The corpse's remaining tissue begins to melt into the ground, leaving only the skeletal remains and what's called a *volatile fatty acid stain*. Once that happens, forensic scientists look to bones for clues. Another ARF scientist, Dr. Richard Jantz, developed a computer program that can determine the age, gender, race, and height of a skeleton. His software has been used to identify victims around the world and to provide evidence during criminal trials.

DYING TO GET IN

So, where does ARF get the bodies for the farm? People donate them at the rate of 100 a year. Bodies spend about two years at the farm. Then the bones are cleaned, labeled, and put into the William M. Bass collection, which now holds 1,000 specimens. Want to be sent to the body farm? Just contact the University of Tennessee at Knoxville. As of today, 2,750 people have donated their bodies to ARF. Just don't forget to tell your family. "We will not fight your family for your body," says ARF.

10 SCARY THINGS
TO DO AFTER DARK

· · · · · · · · · · · · · · · · · · · ·

But only if you dare!

1. Sit in your closet with the lights out. Don't make a sound…just listen. After a few minutes, you'll start hearing sounds you may never have heard before.

2. Prop up a flashlight so it shines on a wall. Shape your hands in front of the light to make giant monsters such as Godzilla and other movie beasts. Practice until you can make the monsters fight. Then find an audience and stage a shadow-puppet monster smack-down.

3. String a white sheet on a rope between two trees. Shine a light on the sheet, and use an insect guide to identify the bugs that land on it.

4. Host a horror-movie night. Beforehand, put together a bone-chilling costume. Once the horror starts rolling, excuse yourself for a bathroom break, change into the costume, and burst back into the room. Terrorize the audience for a few seconds, then casually sit down and start munching popcorn. **Warning:** Terror may cause someone to pee on your couch.

5. In complete darkness, take turns with a friend drawing pictures of well-known monsters (Werewolf, Swamp

Thing, Dracula, and so on). Turn on the lights to
see the results.

6. Creep around every room in your house and take
note of which stairs or floorboards make the spookiest
creaks and groans. Then use those spots for a game of
"Hide and Creep." Choose someone to be "It." With
the lights out, players create creaks or groans and
then hide. "It" follows the sounds to find each player.
Whoever gets tagged first becomes the next "It."

7. Grab your brother or sister or a buddy. Find a flashlight
for each of you. Shine the lights under your chins and
make grotesque faces. Whoever laughs first loses.

8. Have a parent hide weird objects around the house or
backyard. Play flashlight hide-and-seek to find them.

9. While stargazing, come up with haunting names for
constellations, such as "the Witch's Cauldron" for the
Big Dipper.

10. Cut off the bottom and cut open one side of large
black plastic trash bags to make black sheets. On
a moonless night, head to a unlit park, field, or big
yard. Divide into teams: Vampires vs. Zombies. Give
a sheet to each Vampire. While Zombies count to
100, Vampires hide beneath the sheets. A Zombie
must pull the sheet off each Vampire (and make it a
Zombie) before the Vampire can grab the Zombie's
ankle (and turn it into a Vampire). The game ends
when everyone is either a Vampire or a Zombie.

URBAN LEGENDS

. . . .

Sometimes, there's truth behind those spooky legends!

WHAT'S UNDER THE BED?

THE STORY GOES: A couple on a road trip rolls into a town late at night. After checking into a hotel, they try to get some sleep, but there's a weird smell in their room that gets worse and worse as the night goes on. In the morning, they complain about the smell. A housekeeper comes to check it out while the couple looks on. The smell seems to be strongest around the bed, so all three of them lift the mattress—only to find a dead body stuffed underneath the bed.

THE TRUTH: Dead bodies have been discovered under hotel beds in Florida, California, Nevada, New Jersey, and Missouri—so this tale is based, at least partly, in fact.

PLAYING WITH THE DEAD

THE STORY GOES: Some teenagers go to the fair and decide to scare themselves silly in the haunted house. While poking around the props inside, they accidentally knock over a "corpse" and discover…it's a real body.

THE TRUTH: The legend may be based on something that happened in the early 1940s. A robber named Elmer McCurdy was killed by a band of outlaws. After the funeral home embalmed him, the undertaker decided to charge people a nickel to see him. Visitors stuffed nickels in McCurdy's mouth for years—until one day, when his "brothers" showed up to claim his body. Actually, the men weren't related to McCurdy. They were carnies searching for a new sideshow prop. McCurdy's body spent years in fun houses, amusement parks, and wax museums before someone discovered he was a real corpse. In 1977, he was finally laid to rest in an Oklahoma cemetery.

THE ALBINO ALLIGATORS

THE STORY GOES: A family from New York City went on vacation in Florida. The kids brought home a suitcase full of adorable baby alligators. But when the alligators got bigger and nastier, the people didn't want to deal with them and so they flushed them down the toilet. Some of the alligators survived and began living and breeding in the sewers, where they produced a race of giant, mutant, albino super-alligators. To this day, albino alligators lurk in New York City's sewer system.

THE TRUTH: In 1935, a newspaper reported that several New York City boys who were shoveling snow into a manhole discovered an alligator in the sewer. After they got the gator out, it snapped at them. The frightened boys killed it with their shovels. Did the alligator actually live in the sewer? Not likely. According to a New York sewer-management worker, there isn't enough food underground for alligators to survive. "The vast majority of it has been, to put it as delicately as possible, pre-digested," he said.

● ● ●

THE BLOB

....

An Uncle John's Eerily Twisted Tale!

SPLASH! SNEED SENT ANOTHER WAVE of water over the side of the bathtub. "Battleship attack!" he said as he used his new model battleship to sink a cruiser.

"Sneed! Are you making a mess in that bathroom?"

"No, Mom!" Sneed hollered.

"Make sure you clean everything, including that tub," barked his mom. "No bathtub rings!"

Splash! "Battleship attack!" said Sneed.

If Sneed hadn't been so busy making a mess in the bathroom, he might have noticed a light streak across the evening sky. He might have made a wish, thinking it was a shooting star. But Sneed would have been very, very wrong. The strange green glowing object landed in the field behind Sneed's house. It lay still for a moment, and then...it began to stretch and ooze and seep toward Sneed's house. It splootched across the yard and squelched up the side of the house to the bathroom window.

As Sneed toweled off, he watched the dirt-scum soapsuds swirl down the drain. "The ring's not that bad," he said. Then the light in the bathroom began to change to a weird glowing green. "Ahh!" yelled Sneed as the green blob flowed over the windowsill and plopped into the bathtub. It coated the sides of the tub until the whole thing glowed green. "Mom!" Sneed yelled. "There's something gross in the bathtub!"

"There's always something gross in the bathtub after you've used it!" his mom yelled back. "Clean that ring!"

There was no way Sneed was getting near that thing. But then, he noticed something. The green blob had his model. It had taken Sneed a whole week to make that battleship. "Gimme that!"

Sneed reached for his model, but the blob oozed over the side of the tub and shot out the bathroom window. Sneed rushed downstairs, towel flapping, and chased the blob along his street. Dogs howled, cats yowled, and people screamed in horror: "Call the police!" "Call the fire department!" "Call the Marines!"

"Gimme back my battleship!" Sneed yelled.

The blob rounded the corner and headed toward Main Street. As it passed the movie theater, it absorbed spilled popcorn tubs and empty soda cups. Then, just before Sneed lost sight of it, it zipped into the grocery store. "Stop that blob. It has my model!" he shouted.

Crash! Bang! Wham! Within seconds, the store manager, the cashier, and a line of customers ran shrieking from the building. They left behind a trail of broken jars, dented cans, and smashed produce. Sneed tracked the blob by the sparkling floor it left in its wake as it absorbed the debris. He caught up with the blob in the frozen-food aisle.

"Frozen-food attack!" he yelled as he chucked bags of frozen corn and carrots and peas at the blob. The blob absorbed bag after bag, growing larger and glowing brighter with each one. "Still won't give me my model?" Sneed sprinted to the produce section and hoisted the biggest watermelon he could find. He lugged it back to the frozen-food aisle and let it fly. "Watermelon attack!"

The blob sucked the watermelon into its ooze, growing bigger and glowing greener. Then it rose up and lunged at Sneed. "Ahhh!" Sneed yelled. He ran past the dairy section and the deli and the meat department until he couldn't run anymore. "I'm done for." Sneed panted. Then he noticed which aisle he was on—the cleaning product aisle. He'd tried everything else. Why not?

"Cleaner attack!" Sneed grabbed a can of Mr. Clean and starting spraying the blob. This time, instead of getting bigger, the blob burped and whistled like a balloon losing air. Pretty soon, the blob had shrunk to the size of a frozen pea.

"That's the end of you," Sneed told the pea-size blob as he picked up his battleship. Outside the store, a crowd waved and cheered. Sneed took a bow.

"Sneed!" His mom ran in. "They told me you were fighting a green-blob monster! Are you okay?"

"I'm fine, Mom," Sneed told her.

"And how did you get our tub so clean? It sparkles."

Sneed's eyes widened. For the first time, he really noticed how clean the store was after the blob's "attack." He scooped up the pea blob. "So that's what you were up to!" He closed his fist around the pea blob and raised it high. "You and me, buddy. Bathtub-ring attack!"

THE END

BATHROOM SHRIEKS

·····················

When you gotta go…go with the "E-e-e-ek!"

• **GLOW-IN-THE-DARK TOILET PAPER.** Avoid the blinding glare of bright lights on nighttime bathroom visits with toilet paper that glows eerily green in the dark. Also useful for power outages, camping trips, and glow-in-the-dark mummy costumes. ($6.99)

• **BLOOD-BATH SHOWER CURTAIN.** If the bloody handprints smeared down the front of this shower curtain don't make you think of *Psycho*—Alfred Hitchcock's classic horror movie—then you're probably not allowed to see R-rated movies yet. Trust us when we say this curtain will make your parents' hearts pound. ($19.99. Matching bloody-footprint bath mat sold separately.)

• **SKELETON TOILET-PAPER HOLDER.** A hollow-eyed skeleton grins above bony hands that helpfully hold a T.P. roll between them. ($13.55)

• **ZOMBIE-HAND TOILET TOPPER.** Looks like a rotting hand coming up out of a blood-filled toilet bowl. To use, just peel off the backing and stick it to the lid. It's removable (so maybe Mom won't kill you). And reusable (so you can scare Dad's socks off, too!). ($5.52)

THE HAIRY TRUTH

. . . .

Legends say that to become a werewolf, you have to be
bitten by one. Medical science begs to differ.

WOLFING OUT

In 2009, Dr. Ken Walker came home from a
vacation in the Caribbean with what looked like a really
good tan. Then his finger and toenails started falling
off. Dark bristly hair sprouted along his cheekbones.
Was Walker turning into a werewolf? No. But he had
a condition that may be where werewolf legends came
from. It's called *porphyria cutanea tarda*, and it's a blood
disease with symptoms that may sound familiar to
werewolf (and vampire) enthusiasts.

DARK NEWS

Porphyria sufferers are highly sensitive to light. Going
out during the day can cause blisters or even burns to
the skin. As the burns heal, they leave scars. Sometimes
hair begins to grow on the scarred areas, especially on
the face. The hair growth may be the body's way of
protecting the skin from more damage.

Luckily for Dr. Walker, he lives in an age when
the body's biochemistry is understood. If he'd been born
before the 1900s, he might have been hunted down as
a werewolf. "I turned into a strange-colored man with

weird facial hair who had to avoid the sun," Dr. Walker said. "No wonder porphyria is often thought to be the medical condition behind such myths as werewolves and vampires."

BLOODY CLUES

The disease is caused when the body doesn't have enough of a certain kind of enzyme in the liver. That enzyme converts *porphyrins* (natural red and purple pigments found in animals and plants) into *heme* (part of the oxygen-carrying hemoglobin in blood cells). Instead of changing, porphyrins pile up until they reach toxic levels.

The disease isn't passed to its victims by a wolf bite. Triggers include certain drugs, smoking, and excess drinking (in Dr. Walker's case, wine was the culprit). Too much stress, fasting, and chemicals can also cause red and purple pigment pileups. The final trigger? Exposure to the sun. (Yikes!)

• • •

Dinner was served for three
At Dracula's house by the sea,
The *hors d'oeuvres* were fine,
But I choked on my wine
When I learned that the main course was me!

—lyrics from *Dinner with Drac* by John Zacherle

BEASTLY BIG

. . . .

We're really glad the Ice Age ended 10,000 years ago. Why? Because of the super-sized animals. See how many beasts you can match with their descriptions.

1. Eight feet long and heavier than today's black bears, these water-dwellers had six-inch teeth that looked like a hippo's.

2. These 800-pounders would lie in wait for camels or mastodons to lumber by. Then they'd spring from the bushes and sink their 10-inch-long canine teeth into their victims' necks.

3. They hunted in packs and used their massive rear teeth for tearing off chunks of flesh and crushing bones. Then they swallowed those chunks of bison or giant sloths whole.

4. On its hind legs, the largest and most powerful Ice Age land predator in North America stood 11.5 feet tall. It had powerful upper-body strength and long arms ending in 8-inch claws: the better to reach out and slash open whatever it wanted to eat.

5. This Ice Age fatty waddled in at 4,000 lbs. Bony shielding covered most of its body and protected it from predators. So did the massive mace-like club on the end of its tail.

A. saber-tooth cats,
B. giant short-faced bear,
C. giant beavers, **D.** the gigantic armadillo-like glyptodon, **E.** dire wolves.

Answers on page 286.

TURN A HAT
INTO A HORROR

· ·

Need to wear something terrifying on your head?
Don't worry—Uncle John's got you covered.

BLOODY EYEBALL HAT
WHAT YOU NEED: Any type of hat, an old ping-pong ball, markers, a sharp pencil, about 6 inches of thin red ribbon, a needle and thread
WHAT TO DO: Draw an iris and pupil on the ping-pong ball and color them in. Add red squiggles around the iris to make the eyeball look bloodshot. Carefully poke a small hole into the opposite side of the eyeball with the pencil. Tie a knot or two at one end of the red ribbon, and use the pencil to push the knot through the hole so it's inside the eyeball. (The ball should hang if you hold the opposite end of the ribbon.) Thread the needle and secure it to the free end of the red ribbon. Sew that end of the ribbon onto the top of your hat so that the bloody eyeball hangs down. Tie a tight knot when you're done.

THE GHOST HEAD

WHAT YOU NEED: White stocking cap with rounded (not pointed) top, scissors, black felt, and fabric glue
WHAT TO DO: Cut two black ovals out of the felt.

They'll be your ghost's eyes. Glue the eyes near the top of the hat. Your ghost hat is done! Pull the cap down over your forehead and the ghost floats on your head.

SKULL HAT VARIATION: Want to make a skull instead of a ghost? No problem. Keep the black felt eyes. Also cut two narrow nose strips and three or four rectangular teeth from the black felt. Glue the nose strips close together below the eyes and the teeth evenly spaced along the bottom of the hat.

ZOMBIE BARBIE HAT

WHAT YOU NEED: An old hat with a wide sturdy brim, a few Barbie-type dolls that have seen better days, fine-tip markers, scissors, and strong craft glue.

WHAT TO DO: First, pull off the dolls' heads. (Sorry, Barbies!) Rip some hair from each head to give it that "undead head" look. Use the markers to draw stitches on the dolls' foreheads, darken their eyes, and put red squiggles around their faces so they look like they're dripping blood. Glue the heads around the hat brim. Let the glue dry for several hours.

BODY-PARTS VARIATION: If fewer Barbies are available, try a little dismemberment. Pull off arms and legs as well as heads. Use the markers to zombify the body parts, and then glue them to the hat brim.

• • •

FEAR FACTOR: Estimated number of documented Bigfoot sightings since 1958: 1,500.

SCARY-STUPID CRIMINALS

∙ ∙

It's hard to believe crooks can be this dumb.
But—believe us—they can.

SORRY...WE'RE CLOSED

On April 4, 2012, Olga Perdomo walked into the
Albany Bank and Trust on West Lawrence Avenue in
Chicago and handed a note to one of the tellers. The
time: 5:00 p.m. The note demanded "all of your money,
no cops, no dye pack." After reading the note, the quick-
thinking teller told the woman that 5:00 p.m. was closing
time and she'd have to come back the next day. The woman
left the bank, empty-handed. She was arrested a few days
later when she was spotted outside the bank once again.

PLUMB DUMB

At about 1:30 on a Thursday afternoon, Utica, New
York, police responded to a report of a bank robbery
in progress. It was the third attempted robbery of the
day, and this perp had the same MO. He screamed
obscenities, demanded that bank employees put money
in a bag, and threatened them with...the sticky end of a
toilet plunger. Police chased down and arrested 49-year-old
Lawrence Deptola. His "weapon" was found in the bank.

CAUGHT ON CAMERA

When Roderick Ward of Newton County, Georgia, returned home from a 10-day trip, he spotted something odd—a dog collar in the bathroom. Ward doesn't have a dog. "There was dog hair everywhere, so I was like, 'Somebody done wash the dog in my house!'" Ward told police. Besides bathing their dog, the burglars had also hosted a birthday party. The evidence? Ward found a half-eaten birthday cake in his kitchen and a camera full of party pictures they'd left behind. Police identified two teens and a young child in the photos and contacted their parents. After the parents apologized—and returned two other cameras and his spare house keys—Ward decided not to press charges.

EAT THE EVIDENCE

An unidentified prowler shattered a window of a parked Jeep near the University of Washington, but didn't steal anything. Instead, the vandal left behind something for the car's owner—a dozen tortillas scattered across the floorboard. Befuddled by the break-in, police reportedly said, "The Seattle Police Department would like to take this opportunity to remind car prowlers that you shouldn't break into something that's nachos."

• • •

"On a New York subway you get fined for spitting, but you can throw up for nothing."—**Lewis Grizzard**

NO-NOGGIN GOBLINS

....

These ghosts have lost more than their lives.
They've lost their heads!

HEADLESS ANNE. King Henry VIII of England wanted a son to be his heir to the throne. Anne Boleyn didn't produce one. So the king accused her of witchcraft and threw her into the Tower of London, and then had her beheaded. Boleyn was executed on May 19, 1536. Some say that every year, on the anniversary of her death, Anne rides in a ghostly coach across eleven bridges near London, clutching her severed head.

KNITTING BEAUTY. No crops will grow in the Sourlands region of central New Jersey. Why? Legend says the land is cursed by the headless ghost of "Knitting Betty." Elizabeth "Betty" Wert lived in the Sourlands during the American Revolution. Her fiancé answered George Washington's call to arms and headed off to fight the Redcoats. Day after day, Betty sat atop a rocky outcropping knitting as she waited for his return. Her beau never came home, and Betty wanted revenge. She became a spy for Washington's Continental Army. When the Brits caught her, they chopped off her head. Seems Betty made it back home to the Sourlands. Some see a gorgeous ghost with flowing brunette hair dressed in a long blue dress. She sits on what is now called Knitting Betty's Rock, patiently knitting as she waits. Others see a headless woman sitting on the rock. Her restless head spins and spins in her lap.

THE HEADLESS FRENCHMAN. The French pioneer Étienne Brulé explored Pennsylvania from 1614 to 1618. He was looking for silver. But in an area known as the Twin Sisters, he found something else: angry natives who wanted the white men out of their territory. Brulé's party was attacked, and one of his men was beheaded. Indian legend says that the headless Frenchman returns at midnight on the full moon every October, carrying his head under one arm.

THE SCREAMING SKULL. A man named Roger Downes was killed during a drunken brawl on Tower Bridge in London in the mid-1600s. His head was cut off, and his body thrown into the River Thames. But someone was kind enough to send his head to his sister. She lived at her family's mansion, Wardley Hall. For some ghastly reason, she decided to display the head on the top step of a staircase. In time, the flesh rotted away, leaving only the skull. Downes's relatives no longer live in the hall, but new owners just can't get rid of his skull. It screams in protest when moved (or disrespected, according to one guest). The skull has been buried, burned, and smashed. Yet it always ends up back in its place on the stairs.

DEAD ZONES

· ·

Huge areas in the world's waters now have almost no life.
No fish swimming. No seaweed waving. Here's the story.

DEAD ZONE: The Gulf of Mexico
The zone in the Gulf of Mexico changes from year to year, but sometimes it's as big as 8,500 square miles. (That's the size of New Jersey!)

THE VICTIMS: Fish, turtles, and other sea creatures

THE CULPRIT: Fertilizer runoff from farmland in U.S. states along the Mississippi River. Fertilizer used in modern farming is loaded with nitrogen. Nitrogen promotes huge "blooms" of algae: Millions of the tiny plant-like organisms fill the water. When algae die, they sink to the bottom. Microbes gobble them up and form "bacterial mats" that release toxic gases. The result: not enough oxygen for fish and other aquatic creatures to breathe. They leave the area or suffocate to death.

CHANCE OF RECOVERY: Weather can affect the size of the Gulf's dead zone. In 2011, scientists expected the zone to reach its largest size ever because of the considerable flooding that spring along the Mississippi. But high winds from Tropical Storm Don churned up the water, helping to replenish some of the oxygen. The dead zone remained huge, but it didn't reach the record size that was anticipated. A year later, in 2012, very dry weather caused a drought in farming regions along the Mississippi, and the dead zone was reduced to about 3,000 square miles—less than half its usual size. Scientists were mildly encouraged to see such a big effect from just one season of reduced nitrogen from fertilizer runoff. "If we could find some way to stop all that nitrate from going down the river, the problem would be solved in a year or two," said an aquatic ecologist from the University of Michigan.

DEAD ZONE: The Black Sea
In the 1980s, this zone was the largest in the world—the size of Switzerland.

THE VICTIMS: Mussels, crabs, fish, sea grasses

THE CULPRIT: Detergents from wastewater, fertilizers, air pollution. During the 1960s, '70s, and '80s, the flow of nitrogen and phosphorus into Europe's Danube River doubled. Most came from fertilizer, air pollution, and detergents in wastewater from cities in Communist countries such as East Germany, Romania, Bulgaria, and Hungary. In 1989, Communism collapsed. Fertilizer became so expensive, farmers had to cut down on its use. Within a few years, the dead zone had mostly disappeared.

CHANCE OF RECOVERY: "It's a clear first—a successful reversal of dead zones," says Andrew Hudson, of UN Oceans, an environmental group established by the United Nations. As the Black Sea became healthier, many species rebounded. The fertilizer reductions were unintentional, but the countries recognized the benefits and have worked to reduce other forms of pollution.

PUMPKIN GAMES

・・・・・・・・・・・・・・・・・・・・・

Even when it's not Halloween, pumpkins have their uses!

PIG SHOOT. Paint a few pumpkins to look like Angry Birds and a few more to look like the birds' mortal enemies—pigs! That's what 12-year-old Sam Beards did. The budding British engineer used a compressed air cannon to blast pumpkin Birds at pumpkin Pigs propped up on planks on the other side of a field. "It's great fun, and beats the Internet version by a mile," Sam says. But don't get in their way: these Birds fly at up to 500 mph.

PUMPKIN DROP. Every year, Society of Physics students at Harvard College test Isaac Newton's Theory of Gravity. How? "By throwing pumpkins off a roof," explained SPS vice president, Tom S. Rice. First they use liquid nitrogen to freeze the pumpkins. Then they climb to the top of the Jefferson Building on campus, and...*Banzai!* They drop the pumpkins. Witnesses say pumpkins frozen using liquid nitrogen burst "with a satisfying 'pop' into hundreds of still-smoking shards."

PUMPKIN BOWLING. Folks in Minnesota save their pumpkin fun for New Year's Day. They store a few fall pumpkins in the freezer. Come winter, they fill empty plastic-soda bottles with water and stick them in a snowbank to freeze. Then they shovel off a driveway, set up the frozen pop bottles like bowling pins, and...hurl a rock-hard frozen pumpkin toward them. *Strike!*

CHUNK A PUNKIN. In the 1980s, John Ellsworth, a blacksmith in Bridgeville, Delaware, liked to test his strength against that of his friends. How? They threw the anvils lying around his shop. "It's a tricky game, and a young man's one at that," Ellsworth said. "We got so we could still do it, but it hurt." When he hit his thirties, Ellsworth decided to stop flinging anvils and build a catapult to launch...pumpkins! There are four basic rules for a Punkin Chunkin' contest: 1) the pumpkin must weigh at least 8 pounds, 2) it can't split apart until it hits the ground, 3) the catapult can't cross the throwing line, and 4) the pumpkins can't be stuffed with anything (like straw, or metal, or...explosives). The pumpkin that flies the farthest wins. Punkin Chunkin' may be the only pumpkin sport with its very own theme song:

> Mine eyes have seen the glory of the
> flinging of the gourd,
> Which began years ago by some
> guys who were a little bored.
> As they shot their fateful pumpkins they cried,
> "Let me win, Dear Lord."
> Their hope is ever strong.
> Glory, Glory, Punkin Chunkin'
> Their hope is ever strong.
> —**Sheila Cicchi (also known as Brownielocks)**

NIGHT OF
THE LIVING DEAD

· ·

This monster tale is true!

IT WAS A DARK AND STORMY NIGHT . . .
One dreary night in 1816, a handful of writers
huddled by a fire, listening to a storm rage outside. The
friends often got together to read ghost stories, but on
this night, one of them—a poet named Lord Byron—
challenged the others to a scary-story writing contest. They
all took pen to paper and began, but only one of them ever
finished. She was the youngest writer in the room—just 19
years old—and her name was Mary Shelley.

Mary's spooky tale was published as a novel two
years later. The book was so terrifying, many people
doubted that a teenage girl could have written it. Some
thought her husband—a poet named Percy—wrote
it. (He didn't.) The story *is* grisly—it's about a scientist
named Victor who builds a creature by fusing dead bodies
together. Everyone the monster meets treats him cruelly,
so he murders the scientist and the scientist's family.

Sound familiar? It should: Mary Shelley's fictional
monster was named after its creator: Victor *Frankenstein*.
Despite all of its gruesome parts (or maybe because of
them), *Frankenstein* became a huge success.

A DARK AND STORMY NIGHT . . . THE SEQUEL

Mary Shelley died in 1851, but if she were alive today, she'd probably be proud of the legacy her novel has left behind. *Frankenstein* has been adapted dozens of times into plays, movies, comics, songs, commercials, video games, and other books.

Some of the most popular movie adaptations feature actor Boris Karloff playing the monster. Karloff starred as the creature in three films during the 1930s: *Frankenstein, Bride of Frankenstein,* and *Son of Frankenstein.* In each of the movies, he's dressed as a tall hulking man-like monster with a broad forehead and clamps coming out of his neck. To play the part, Karloff wore four-inch platform shoes that weighed in at 26 pounds. He also had a square-shaped block stuck to his skull by makeup artists. The block was designed by artist Jack Pierce, who spent months studying anatomy and surgery for inspiration.

"I figured that Frankenstein, who was a scientist but no practicing surgeon, would take the simplest way [to] put in a brain. That is the reason I decided to make the monster's head square and flat like a shoebox and dig that big scar across his forehead with the metal clamps holding it together," said Pierce.

Karloff did not enjoy dressing up for the part. "I spent three and a half hours in the makeup chair getting ready for the day's work," he said. "The makeup itself was quite painful. There were days when I thought I would never be able to hold out until the end of the day!"

ATTACK OF
THE KILLER PEANUT

• • • • • • • • • • • • • • • • • • • •

An Uncle John's Eerily Twisted Tale!

SOME PEOPLE THINK my life is terrifying. Why? Because I see things nobody else can see. Don't get me wrong. I don't see dead people everywhere (or anywhere, for that matter). I don't see ghosts or zombies or werewolves or vampires. Nope. I see how people will die.

Let me give you an example. Yesterday, I was at the grocery store with my mom. At the checkout line, I looked at the girl who rang up our groceries. She was probably only a few years older than I am. She was smiling at us, scanning bags of frozen peas, and asking how our day was going. Then I saw an elephant stomp on her face. I kid you not. An elephant! As we left the store, I leaned in close and whispered, "This is very important—watch out for elephants." She looked at me as if I was crazy. I get that a lot.

People who know about my ability usually ask me all the same questions, so I'll just answer them for you right now:

1. Can you see your own death?
No.

2. Do you see everyone's death?

No, and I don't have much control over it.

3. Can people's deaths be changed?

Now that's the million-dollar question.

For years, I've been worrying about my best friend, Kaia. When we met, I saw a vision of her keeling over in the cafeteria after eating a peanut. I told her about it right away because she didn't look much older in the vision. She thought I was crazy. "Alicia," she said. "I'm not even allergic to peanuts."

"Are you sure?" I asked. "You might want to get that checked out."

"Of course I'm sure! I eat peanut butter like every single day!"

"Well, I think you're going to develop a peanut allergy soon. This is important! You cannot let a peanut kill you!" I kind of yelled the last part, and people in the hallway started staring at us, so I eased up after that.

But I still got nervous at lunchtime, especially when Kaia wore her favorite pink shirt. It was the shirt she was wearing in my vision, so I just knew her peanut allergy was going to strike when she had it on. She thought it was funny that I got so nervous, so she would go out of her way to drive me crazy.

"Mmmmm," she would say as she took a gigantic bite of peanut-butter sandwich. Then she would pretend to grab her throat and fall dead on the ground. She did this so often that I started to feel a little less scared, especially when no peanuts were in sight. So I wasn't concerned on the day we shared a bag of trail mix at lunch, even though she was wearing her pink shirt. I scooped out a handful of dried cherries and chocolate chips and passed the bag to Kaia. "Did you do your English homework?" I asked.

She shoveled some trail mix into her mouth and mumbled something unintelligible before passing the bag back to me.

I rooted around for more chocolate chips. "Hmm?" I mumbled. No reply, so I keep rooting.

Then Kaia smacked me on the shoulder. I looked up. Her face was blue. I looked down at the bag again. There were peanuts in the trail mix!

I jumped to my feet. "Allergies!" I shrieked. "Help!"

Kaia shook her head desperately and grabbed my shirt. She pointed to her throat. I wondered why she wasn't talking. Then it hit me—she wasn't allergic! She was choking!

"Holy peanut butter!" I said. "Dial 911! Emergency!" I waved my arms and then sprang into action. A few months earlier, a Red Cross representative had come to school to teach us first aid, including the Heimlich maneuver—but did I remember how to do it?

I grabbed Kaia from behind and clasped my hands at her upper belly. I pushed as hard as I could. Nothing happened. Kaia started drooping toward the floor. You saw this coming, I thought. Now you have to change it.

I pushed one more time as hard as I could and watched a spit-covered peanut fly out of Kaia's mouth.

She dropped to the floor and gasped.

"Are you okay?!" I cried.

Kaia wheezed for another minute, then she managed a weak smile and reached up to put a hand on my shoulder. "Told you I wasn't allergic to peanuts," she rasped.

THE END

• • •

MONSTER MANIA

A few riddles about our favorite monsters.

Q: What do you get when you cross the Swamp Thing with peanut butter?
A: Something disgusting that sticks to the roof of your mouth.

Q: What is the Loch Ness Monster's favorite meal?
A: Fish and ships.

Q: How can you tell if Godzilla is a meat-eater or a plant-eater?
A: Lie down on a plate and see what happens.

Q: Do zombies smell as rotten as they look?
A: Only a phew.

Q: What kind of tablet did the Cyclops buy?
A: An iPad.

Q: What did Count Dracula say when his son kept asking riddles?
A: You drive me batty!

Q: Who attends plays at Pyramid Elementary?
A: Mummies and Deadies.

DÍA DE LOS MUERTOS

. . . .

A special day to party with the dead!

FIVE HUNDRED YEARS AGO, Spanish Conquistadors showed up in what is now Mexico. They found the natives mocking death with a month-long celebration. The party was presided over by the goddess *Mictecacihuatl*, the "Lady of the Dead." Seems the native peoples believed the souls of the dead returned each year to enjoy the company of living relatives.

The Spanish did their best to stop the practice, but had to settle for shortening the celebration. *Día de los Muertos* (Day of the Dead) now spans November 1–2. Families decorate gravesites of deceased relatives with flowers—the brighter the better—and with candles… lots and lots of candles. And they bring food: iced *pan de muertos* (Day of the Dead bread) shaped like leaves or cats or ducks, and yummy sugar skulls. Each skull has the name of a dead relative on its forehead and gets eaten to remember the deceased.

Hispanic families in the United States party with the dead, too. "We offer incense and flowers. We play their favorite music, make their favorite food," said Arizona artist Zarco Guerrero. But watch out partygoers! The Walt Disney Company is trying to trademark "Día de los Muertos" for a movie due out in 2015.

THE GROSS GOURMET

. . . .

One person's gross-out is another person's delicacy.

- In Japan, digger wasps aren't just insects that sting and paralyze their prey—they're a tasty treat! About 120 miles outside of Tokyo, digger wasps are harvested, boiled, and then baked (bodies intact) into wafer-thin wasp crackers! (Yum!)

- Two canned foods top the delicacy lists in Korea and Thailand: canned chrysalis (the shell in which a caterpillar becomes a butterfly) and canned scorpion.

- "Bishop's nose" is a favorite treat in Manila, the Phillipines. What is it? Chicken butt—it's the fattest part of the chicken, and fat makes anything taste good.

- In the Appalachian Mountains of the U.S., squirrel brains have been on the menu for decades. Warning: eating squirrel brains has been linked to a form of mad cow disease, so this delicacy is not recommended.

- *Casu Marzu* might win the award for "grossest food ever." It's a cheese made in the region of Sardinia in Italy. What makes it so tasty? Maggots. These fly larva are allowed on the cheese to help ferment or create it. But then they stick around—even when the cheese is eaten. Maggot cheese has been officially outlawed, but if you can deal with larva jumping off your meal—up to 6 inches high—*Bon appétit!*

HAPPY HOWL-O-WEEN!

. . . .

Some Halloween costumes are just really bad ideas.

PERMANENT PIRATE

There are ways to attach a pirate's eyepatch that aren't harmful, like tying it around your head or sticking it on with eyelash glue. In 2010, one 45-year-old man thought he had a better idea: using Super Glue to add the finishing touches to his pirate costume. He wound up in the emergency room with an eyepatch superglued to his face.

SNAGGLETOOTH

In 2004, a 10-year-old girl wasn't content with the bite-on plastic fangs that most Halloween costume stores sell. She thought it would be cooler to glue plastic fangs on top of her real front teeth. It took an emergency trip to the dentist to pry these fangs off.

BARBECUED SHEEP

When a 28-year-old Lewiston, Maine, man made his own sheep costume for Halloween, he thought cotton balls would make perfect sheep's wool. They did—until he brushed up against someone smoking a cigarette at a party. He found out the hard way that cotton balls aren't fire resistant. The costume went up in flames. And the sheered sheep went to the hospital for burn treatment.

SLICK HAIR

When her son decided to dress up as a vampire for Halloween, a woman in New Bedford, Massachusetts, used Vaseline to slick down his hair. It worked very well—until she tried to wash it off. "I must have washed his hair five hundred times," she said. The problem: Vaseline is waterproof. "I just kept washing his head and washing his head," said Mom. "He was miserable."

KNOCK, KNOCK . . .

When someone knocked on her classroom door in 2011, a Massachusetts high school teacher asked a 15-year-old student to open it. Outside the door: a man in a mask carrying what looked like a running chainsaw. The student freaked. He jumped back, tripped, fell, and broke his kneecap. The jokester? Another teacher. The punchline? The student's family sued for $100,000.

THIS UNCLE STINKS!

During a 2012 Halloween bash, a Pennsylvania man spotted what he thought was a skunk lying motionless in the yard, grabbed his shotgun, and...shot it. Problem? It wasn't a skunk. It was his 9-year-old niece. The kids at the party had been outside playing a game of hide-and-seek. The victim was wearing a black costume with a black hat sporting a white feather tassel. She's going to recover. He's going on trial for assault and reckless endangerment.

●   ●   ●

DAY CREATURE

BY MICHELLE R. WEAVER

THE CRUEL, COILED MOUTH PARTS UNRAVEL AS IT PREPARES TO SUCK THE LIFE OUT OF ITS NEXT VICTIM!

ITS UNBLINKING SOULLESS EYES TARGET ITS PREY! READY TO DEVOUR, IT SWOOPS DOWN!

SWOOP

HOW TO MAKE A SHRUNKEN HEAD

. . . .

You'll probably never use this recipe, but you can still hold it over your kid brother or sister's (ahem) head.

A HUNDRED YEARS AGO, the Jivaro (hee-var-o) tribes living deep in the jungles of Ecuador and Peru collected the heads of their enemies and turned them into trophies. Here's how they did it…step by step.

STEP 1: FIND A HEAD. Peel the skin away from the skull (hair and all). Sew the eye and mouth openings closed (to trap the soul inside so it won't haunt you). Turn the head inside out. Scrape away the fat using a sharp knife.

STEP 2: COOK THE HEAD. Add jungle herbs to a pot of water and bring to a boil. Add the head and simmer for one to two hours. Remove the head from the water.

STEP 3: SHRINK THE HEAD. Fill the head with hot stones, rolling it constantly to prevent scorching. Repeat with smaller and smaller pebbles as the head shrinks. Mold the facial features between each step.

STEP 4: GIVE THE HEAD A FACIAL. Hang the head over the fire to dry. Once dry, polish it with ashes. Moisturize with berries to prevent the head from cracking. Sew the neck hole closed and trim the hair.

PRANKED!

....

April Fools' Day only comes once a year. But why wait?
These pranks work year-round.

Peek-a-Boo!

This one is a classic. Hide behind a closed door and wait for your victim to approach. When the door opens, jump forward and make an outrageous noise. Works every time! (**Duh Alert:** Don't hide behind a door that opens toward you unless you want to get smacked in the face.)

EEK! A SPIDER

You'll need a fake spider for this prank—the bigger and hairier the better. Use strong tape to attach a long piece of string to the spider's body. Tie the other end to a sturdy stick or pole. Quietly approach your victim from behind (this works best if he or she is watching TV or engrossed in a book or video game). Dangle the spider and let it settle on your victim's shoulder.

HELLO?

Start watching a scary movie with friends or family. When a truly terrifying scene is approaching, slip silently out of the room. Use a cell phone to call the home line or the cell of someone who is still watching. When he or she answers, make your voice low and creepy and breathy, and say, "Are you watching me? I'm watching you...."

MONSTER UNDER THE BED

Just before bedtime, crawl under a sibling's bed and find a comfortable position. (If you share a room, make a show of turning in first. Stuff your bed with pillows so it looks like you're sleeping.) Once your brother or sister is in bed, wait in silence a few minutes and then start making soft guttural noises. If you're very good at disguising your voice, growl out the person's name followed by creepy sound effects. For maximum fear factor, start very softly so you can barely be heard, and then get louder bit by bit.

THE SPRINTING CANDY

Find a long clear piece of fishing line or strong transparent thread. Tie it around a fun-size candy bar and place the candy on the floor. Hold the other end of the fishing line and find a place to hide that will allow you a view of the candy. When someone tries to pick up the candy, give the line a jerk. Keep going until your victim catches on.

WHEN YOU GOTTA GO . . .

Open the lid of the toilet. Tape an old Halloween mask (the scarier the better) to the inside of the toilet lid. Shut the toilet lid, and then keep your ears open for screams. (**Duh Alert:** If you forget the mask is there and need to go before anyone else does, you'll be the one screaming!)

OUT FOR BLOOD

....

Why is everyone so obsessed with vampires?
We have no idea, but fangs for asking!

VAMPIRE STORIES have been around for
thousands of years. An ancient Babylonian and
Assyrian myth from around 4,000 B.C. describes an
ekimmu (or *edimmu*). What's that? It's a person who
did not receive a proper burial or died a violent death.
Instead of remaining dead, an *ekimmu* returns to suck
the life out of a living human. Here are a few more bits
of vampire lore from human history.

* During the 16th century (1500s), gravediggers checked
  to make sure corpses had not chewed on their burial
  shrouds. Why? It was a sure sign of vampirism. If such
  a sign was seen, the gravedigger would shove a rock or
  brick into the corpse's mouth to keep it from feeding
  on other dead bodies and rising from the grave. In
  2006, scientists found the skull of a female "vampire"
  near Venice, Italy. A slab of rock had been shoved into
  her mouth so forcefully it broke her teeth.

* Drinking the ashes of a burned vampire has been
  said to help those bitten by vampires. But in Russian
  folklore, vampire attacks could be prevented by eating
  bread baked with vampire blood.

- Burying corpses facedown was once a popular way to prevent supposed vampires from coming back to life. If they "woke up," they would dig themselves deeper into the earth instead of clawing their way out. Skeletons thought to be thousands of years old have also been found staked, decapitated, pinned with arrows, and crushed by boulders...all thought to be ways to keep vampires from rising from their graves.

- Garlic is the most traditional way of repelling vampires. It has been used for more than 2,000 years.

- According to a legend from the Balkans, vampires could be born out of fruit that was more than 10 days old (or fruit not eaten by Christmas).

- Vampire hunters in Romania and Hungary had a strange way of finding them. They would lead a horse through a graveyard. If the horse refused to step over a grave, a vampire rested inside the grave.

- Nineteenth-century Transylvanian midwives knew how to stop the dead from turning into vampires. They drove nails into a corpse's forehead before burial or cut off its head and stuffed its mouth with garlic.

- Count Von Count from *Sesame Street* comes by his love of counting honestly. Folklore says vampires love counting. And if they're tricked into counting a *lot* of something—say, seeds or grains of sand—they will forget all about drinking your blood.

GOING, GOING...
STILL GOING

· ·

Bathroom lore can be scary weird. Cool, huh?

WHEN YOU'VE GOTTA GO

Nineteen-year-old Dylan DiFalco was arrested by sheriff's deputies in Collier County, Florida, after he tripped a busboy who was chasing his friend (the friend was trying to leave without paying). On the way to jail, DiFalco told one of the deputies he needed to go to the bathroom. "Try and hold it like an adult," the officer told him. DiFalco didn't: He peed in the back seat. Then the teen said, "I told you I had to go, you stupid cop." Not smart: the soggy DiFalco was charged with battery (against the busboy) and locked up on a $2,000 bond.

TROOPERS BUST POOPER

When nature called, Wayne Cosney stopped by the side of a road in Defuniak Springs, Florida, to...uhm...go number two. A witness must have thought that was a crappy thing to do. He photographed the event and then contacted police. Authorities responded to investigate and discovered that the car Cosney was driving had been listed as stolen. Cosney's illegal pit stop got him busted for DUI, indecent exposure, and grand theft auto.

GET OFF THE POT

Ness County Sheriff Bryan Whipple (his real name) said a man called his office to report that something was wrong with his girlfriend. She would not get off the toilet. Police found the 35-year-old woman not only sitting on the toilet, but stuck there. "She was not glued," said Whipple. "She was not tied. She was just physically stuck by her body." In fact, the woman's skin seemed to have grown around the seat. "We pried the toilet seat off with a pry bar, and the seat went with her to the hospital," Whipple said. "The hospital removed it." The boyfriend told investigators he'd brought his girlfriend food and water and asked her to come out of the bathroom every day...for two years! Her daily reply? "Maybe tomorrow." The boyfriend had no explanation for why he waited so long to call for help.

THANKS, BUDDY!

In 2008, Gokhan Mutlu got a good deal from a friend: a "buddy pass" that allowed him to fly free from San Diego to New York City on JetBlue airlines. About 90 minutes into the flight, what had seemed like a good deal...wasn't. The pilot made Mutlu give up his seat to a flight attendant and sit on the toilet. When Mutlu complained, the pilot reportedly said, "This is my plane, under my command, and you should be grateful for being on board." Then the aircraft hit turbulence. Passengers were told to return to their seats, but Mutlu had no seat to return to. He sued JetBlue for more than $2 million.

HOW TO TALK TO A GHOST

· ·

What if you could witness haunted happenings in your neighborhood and then bring home proof? Here's how.

CAN YOU HEAR ME NOW?

Investigators on TV ghost-hunting shows spend a lot of time asking questions to rooms that look completely empty. What's up with that? The ghost hunter is trying to capture and record an Electronic Voice Phenomenon (EVP)—a ghostly voice that's so faint, it can only be heard later when the recording is played back.

You don't have to be a professional ghost hunter to try it. All you need is a small audio-recording device… and a haunted house.

BEWARE. Ghost-hunting is not for the faint of heart, so never go investigating by yourself. Take along a friend, or assemble a small team. And get your parents' permission. If the investigation will take place anywhere other than your own house (or a friend's), take a trusted adult (or three) with you.

THINK LIKE A SCIENTIST

- Don't trust all ghost stories as fact. Witness accounts of paranormal activity can be exaggerated over time. Stay objective and act as if you are a scientist looking for proof.
- Keep a level head. When you're on a paranormal investigation, it's easy to think every noise, light, or shadow is caused by a ghost. Good investigators look for real-world explanations first. They know that sounds and lights that come in from the outside—such as people talking, car headlights, and the wind—can fool people into thinking they've encountered a spirit.
- Don't horse around during the investigation. And know where your team members are at all times. Remember: The more professional you act, the better your chances of success.

ATTEMPT TO MAKE CONTACT

- Once you've found a place that is reported to be haunted, you'll have to set up a time to go in at night. Ghosts are said to be most active when all is dark and the rest of the world is asleep. Turn off the lights and use a flashlight only when you need to. Let your eyes get used to the dark.
- Turn on your recorder and lay it on a flat surface. In your normal voice, say, "Hello, is there anyone in here with me?" (Don't use the word "ghost," or tell them they are dead—they might not know it!) Then be silent for a few moments and look and listen for

anything out of the ordinary.

- If the room gets cold or you hear a strange noise, that may be a sign of paranormal activity. To find out, say, "I can't see or hear you. Are you trying to communicate? Could you make a noise or move an object?" If anything weird happens, verify that it's ghostly by asking the spirit to do it again.

- If you feel like a spirit is in the room, ask it more questions: its name, what it's doing there, or what year it is. Remember: Even if you don't hear a response, it doesn't mean you're not getting one. That's why it's important to remain absolutely quiet except when you're asking questions.

MAKE A FRIEND ... OR GET OUT!

- Ghost hunters say most spirits are harmless, but some people report encountering wicked ones. If you feel a nasty presence, don't panic. But get out of there as quickly as you can. Some ghosts are said to feed off fear, so don't give them anything to eat.

- Give the EVP session about an hour, and then wrap it up. Thank the spirits (if they were nice), and leave them be.

- The next day, listen to your recording very carefully. Make a note of every out-of-the-ordinary noise you picked up. If you did a good job investigating, you might just hear a ghostly answer to one of your questions.

THE TALKING DEAD

Some brainless quotes about zombies.

"Okay, well, you're dead. Which is unusual, because we don't normally see this much activity in a dead person."
—Dr. Bronson, *My Boyfriend's Back* (1993)

"I'd rather die while I'm living than live while I'm dead. "
—Jimmy Buffett

"Blood is really warm, it's like drinking hot chocolate but with more screaming."
—Ryan Mecum, *Zombie Haiku: Good Poetry for Your...Brains*

"Zombies can't believe the energy the living waste on nonfood pursuits."
—Patton Oswalt, comic

"Often, a school is your best bet—perhaps not for education but certainly for protection from an undead attack."
—Max Brooks, *The Zombie Survival Guide*

"It is a truth universally acknowledged that a zombie in possession of brains must be in want of more brains."
—Seth Grahame-Smith, *Pride and Prejudice and Zombies*

"Zombies are the only club that accepts everyone. They don't care what you look like. They don't care how old you are."
—Matt Mogk, head of the Zombie Research Society

SCARY SMART

· ·

A brief look at one of the smartest dudes of our time.

BOY MEETS GIRL

While studying for a doctorate at Cambridge, Stephen Hawking got some dreadful news: he had a disease called *amyotrophic lateral sclerosis*. ALS attacks nerve cells in the brain and spinal cord—the ones that control your muscles. Over time, people with ALS have trouble breathing. Their muscles weaken and waste away. They can't move. They can't speak. In time, they can't even breathe on their own. Most ALS sufferers die within ten years.

Hawking could have packed his bags and gone home. No one would have blamed him. Why didn't he? For one thing, he'd just met a really cute girl and he wanted to ask her out. That turned out well (they got married). In time, Hawking became world-famous, wrote best-selling books such as *A Brief History of Time*, won a bunch of big-shot science awards, and…guest-starred on a hit TV show. (More about that later.)

FACTS ABOUT A BOY

- Stephen Hawking was born on January 8, 1942—the 300th anniversary of the death of another amazing scientist and stargazer: Galileo Galilei, the father of modern astronomy and physics.

- Hawking was a grade-school slacker. At age 9, he was near the bottom of his class. In spite of his poor grades, his teachers and classmates nicknamed him "Einstein."
- Despite mediocre grades in school, Hawking aced the scholarship exams that got him into Oxford. His score on the physics exam? Almost perfect.
- Hawking joined the rowing club at Oxford. That made him popular. But rowing practice took up six afternoons a week. That put him behind on his classwork. Hawking says he used "creative analysis to create lab reports"—in other words, he made stuff up.
- Hawking's Ph.D. is in cosmology. No, that's not the study of make-up, it's the study of the origin and development of the universe.

BOY MEETS D'OH-MEST MAN IN THE UNIVERSE

And now...what you've all been waiting for (or skipped ahead to read): In 1999, Hawking guest-starred in an episode of *The Simpsons* titled "They Saved Lisa's Brain." He almost missed the taping because his wheelchair broke down. Then he was 40 minutes late due to traffic. But it all ended well: Hawking and Homer meet up at Moe's tavern, where they discuss the universe. "Your theory of a donut-shaped universe is intriguing, Homer," Hawking says. "I may have to steal it." The producer said the scene was "a chance to get the world's smartest man and the world's stupidest man in the same place." After the episode aired, Hawking said, "Almost as many people know me from *The Simpsons* as for my science."

TROUBLE DOLL

....

*Tired of worrying? Do what kids from Guatemala do—
make a trouble doll to do the worrying for you.*

WHAT YOU NEED:
- 2 pipe cleaners
- 1 large wooden bead
- 1 fine-tipped marker

- Several bright colors of yarn, embroidery thread, or twine

WHAT TO DO:

1. Slide the wooden bead onto one pipe cleaner. Position the bead at the middle of the cleaner, and then twist the two ends of the cleaner together beneath the bead so that it becomes the doll's "head." (Leave enough of the ends untwisted to become "legs.")

2. Twist the other pipe cleaner around the body to make "arms."

3. Wrap the colored yarn, thread, or twine around the pipecleaner body, arms, and legs to look like clothes.

4. Before bedtime, hold the doll in your hand, close your eyes and repeat three times: "Trouble doll, I give you my worries." State your worries. Then take a deep breath and say, "My troubles are gone!" Put the doll under your pillow and sleep tight!

KNOCK THREE TIMES

· ·

An Uncle John's Eerily Twisted Tale!

JILL HACKLE HAUNTED antique shops every weekend looking for an old desk—and not just any old desk, her mother's desk. When her mom died, the state had auctioned off all their stuff: the books, the furniture, the gnarled skeleton's hand, the skull with the candle sticking out of it, and the fake Crown Jewels of Queen Victoria. They'd even sold her pet rat, Scratcher. At least, that's what Matron told her when Scratcher went missing.

"No pets allowed in the orphanage, anyway, girlie," Matron had sneered.

Jill missed her mother almost more than she could bear. It seemed so unfair that someone who'd spent her whole life studying death couldn't find a way to stay out of its clutches.

"The dead are all around us," Jill's mom had told her. "You can see them if you want to. Most people just don't want to."

But some people did. That's where Jill's mom came in. She conducted seances, turning herself into a bridge between the living and their lost loved ones. If the dead didn't show up, Jill knew just what to do: knock three times.

Her mom's desk was the key. It had two drawers

on the left side and two drawers on the right. But the drawers on the right side were fake. Behind them was a hollow space just big enough for Jill to sit inside. Before a seance, Jill would push the hidden latch that swung the fake drawers open like a door, then slip inside. If her mom rapped three times during the seance but no spirit answered, Jill would rap three times from inside her nook.

Just before the cancer took her, Jill's mom had promised to watch over her, even beyond death.

"But how will I know?" Jill had asked.

"I'll use our special knock."

"Three times?" Jill said.

"Three times," her mother had whispered. And then she'd closed her eyes and gone to sleep...forever.

That's why Jill had to find that desk. And she did, but not in an antique shop. One night, as she tossed and turned on her bony mattress, she heard a knock. *Thump.* Then she heard a second knock. *Thump.* And a third. *Thump!* Jill sat straight up in the bed. The knock seemed to be coming from the other side of the wall. Matron's room! Jill crept into the hall. *Knock. Knock. Knock.* She pressed her ear against Matron's door. *KNOCK. KNOCK. KNOCK.*

She turned the doorknob, as slowly and silently as she could. Then she peered inside. The room was bathed in the warm yellow glow of a single lamp that sat atop... her mother's desk! What was it doing here? Jill glanced over her shoulder. Matron was nowhere in sight, so she crept into the room. *Knock. Knock. Knock.*

"Mom?" Jill eased closer to the desk. "Is that you?"

"Don't be ridiculous!" said a muffled voice. "Now get me out of here!"

Jill recognized that voice. And it wasn't her mother's. "How did you get my mother's desk?"

"I bought it," said the matron. "Now get me out!"

Jill blinked. "But…why? You knew I'd been looking everywhere for it."

"It's not rocket science. You wouldn't be looking so hard unless there was something valuable hidden in here. And I'm going to find it."

Jill shook her head. "No, you're not." She pushed the hidden latch, and the fake drawers swung open.

Matron crawled out. "Finally. Now if you know what's good for you, you'll keep your mouth shut about this."

Scratch. Scratch. Scratch.

Matron's eyes widened. "What was that?"

Scratch. Scratch. Scratch.

"I-it's the desk!" Matron shrieked. "Get that thing out of here. Get it out right now!"

"Whatever you say," said Jill. Back in her room, Jill opened the fake drawers again. She shone the flashlight inside. Two red eyes peered out at her. "So that's where you've been hiding." Jill reached in to pull Scratcher into her arms. Then she crawled back into bed. "'Night, Scratcher." She snuggled into her pillow and rubbed her cheek against the rat's soft fur. *Knock. Knock. Knock.* Jill reached out and patted the desk. "'Night, Mom."

THE END

DARK DESTINATIONS

· ·

Tips for where to take your next scare-cation.

1. PHILADELPHIA, PENNSYLVANIA

Pennsylvania's Eastern State Penitentiary opened in 1829.
It had thick castle-like walls. Guards watched inmates
from tall stone towers. It was designed for one thing: to
change the behavior of inmates through "confinement in
solitude with labor." Prisoners lived, ate, slept, and even
exercised alone. They couldn't leave their cells without
having hoods pulled over their heads so they couldn't
see—or be seen by—another human. Many experts
believe years of solitary confinement caused mental
illness among the prisoners. Some say it led to hauntings.
In 1971, the penitentiary was abandoned. But footsteps
are still heard in empty exercise yards. Wails drift down
deserted corridors. Disembodied laughter splits the cold
silence of Cell Block 12. The "haunted prison" opened in
1994 for nighttime creepfests. Since then, 60 paranormal
investigation teams have visited. Their verdict? The
prison is haunted...probably by the ghosts of past inmates.

2. SALEM, MASSACHUSETTS

In 1692, Salem played host to the now-infamous Witch
Trials. After being found guilty of witchcraft, more than

20 men and women were either hung or pressed to death with heavy stones. Rather than shying away from its sordid past, Salem has embraced it. Every Halloween, the city puts on a parade and hosts haunted cruises and trolley tours. Visitors can see spooky magic shows, join mediums for séances, and experience reenactments of the Salem Witch Trials. Oh, and the modern-day Witches of Salem meet on Salem Commons for a "celebration of loved ones who have crossed over."

3. SAVANNAH, GEORGIA

The Institute of Parapsychology has awarded Savannah the nickname "America's Most Haunted City." To understand the hauntings, you have to know the history. Before the Civil War, Savannah was a major exporter of cotton, nicknamed "White Gold." Warehouses crowded the east end of River Street. Slaves baled and stacked all that cotton. Many died from disease while chained to the walls of those warehouses. Now, ghostly shadows are sometimes seen in the warehouses. Disembodied voices echo inside. Items mysteriously move along floors. Savannah also boasts haunted houses, Civil War forts, and cemeteries. At Bonaventure Cemetery, visitors sometimes see a pack of ghost dogs roaming the graves.

4. TOMBSTONE, ARIZONA

Tombstone started out in the 1870s as a mining camp. Pretty soon the town was overrun with bandits and horse thieves, all of them packing pistols and bent on making trouble. Enter: Marshall Virgil Earp and his brothers, Wyatt and Morgan. On October 26, 1881, Tombstone became the site of the most famous shootout in U.S. history. The cattle-rustling Clanton gang shot it out with the Earp brothers and their buddy Doc Holliday at the O.K. Corral. (Actually, they shot it out between the buildings *near* the corral, but that's splitting hairs.) Three outlaws were killed in the fight, and some visitors report seeing their ghosts haunting the corral. Others claim to feel cold spots outside the corral.

Around Halloween, Tombstone's residents take advantage of its history with daily reenactments of the deadly gunfight and ghost tours. By the way, the gunfight still being talked about more than 130 years later lasted...thirty seconds.

5. NEW ORLEANS, LOUISIANA
Slavery, torture, voodoo, and murder are all part of New Orleans' dark past. And many of its narrow streets and dark alleys are home to ghostly legends. The city's most famous ghost? Marie Laveau: "The Voodoo Queen of New Orleans." Laveau is buried in the St. Louis Cemetery on the edge of the French Quarter. Some say she still grants favors, but first, you must knock three times on her crypt. If you visit during the city's four-day Halloween festivities, you might have to stand in line. While you await the Voodoo Queen's favor, check out the parades and costume parties around the French Quarter, and don't miss the city's Voodoo Museum.

6. NEW YORK CITY, NEW YORK

There's something you may not know about the Big Apple: many of the city's parks started out as cemeteries. Thousands of bodies are estimated to have been buried underneath what is now Washington Square Park in the city's Greenwich Village. Before it became a park, the area served as a potter's field (burial place for the poor) and the site of a public gallows. In the late 1700s, the area was used as a cemetery for yellow fever victims. Most people strolling through the park today have no idea how many skeletons rest beneath their feet.

7. SNAGOV, ROMANIA

Fans of Bram Stoker's *Dracula* might enjoy a visit to this snake-shaped lake north of Bucharest, Romania. A tiny island in the middle of the lake is rumored to be the final resting place of the real-life inspiration for the world's most famous vampire: Vlad Dracula Tepes. Prince Vlad lived in the 1400s and now has a reputation for being one of the cruelest rulers to ever live. Why? He had a habit of skewering his enemies—mostly Turks— on long stakes. In 1456, Vlad fortified the tiny island in the middle of Snagov lake. He built a church, a prison, and a torture chamber on the island. Vlad was rumored to have been buried beneath the floor of the church, but when the grave was dug up in 1931, it was...empty. (Some claim the grave contained a headless torso.) Today, the gravesite is known as "Dracula's Tomb."

• • •

GHOSTS AND ROSES

....

Rock-and-run!

IT WAS 2 A.M. Matt Sorum, the drummer for the rock-and-roll band Guns N' Roses, was in a Hollywood music studio producing an album for another band. The band had just finished recording for the night. That left Sorum and engineer Jim Mitchell alone in the studio. The band had sounded fine while they were recording. But during playback, Sorum and Mitchell heard something odd. "Every time we played back the tape there was this low kind of a voice-rumbling sound," Sorum said.

Mitchell took a break and went to the restroom. When he returned, he looked like he was in shock. "I just saw a ghost," he told Sorum. "This guy walked behind me in the bathroom and then he disappeared." Sorum and Mitchell went back to investigate. "We got right to the door and a voice said, "Don't come in here, you're not invited," said Sorum.

"Out of the left corner of my eye I saw this mass of air that looked like a small cloud floating across the room," said Sorum. The icy cloud ran up his arm and down his body. Sorum and Mitchell packed up. Later, they learned that others had seen the same ghost. In 1991, a headless body had been found behind the building. He's believed to be the one who haunts the studio.

ZOMBIE APOCALYPSE

. . . .

*Zombies are fake, right? The United States government
would never confirm the existence of zombies, right? Right?!*

THE ZOMBIES ARE COMING!
That scary headline appeared above a *real* news story
in September 2012. In the report, the U.S. Department of
Homeland Security warned citizens to be prepared for a
zombie apocalypse! Since when did the U.S. government
believe in zombies? Since…never. But government officials
thought a zombie warning would get people's attention.

The real goal: to publicize National Preparedness
Month and help families prepare for an actual (non-
zombie-related) disaster. Turns out, you'd need the same
things to survive a zombie invasion that you'd need to
survive an earthquake, a hurricane, a disease pandemic,
or a terrorist attack. Homeland Security says families
should keep nonperishable food, bottled water, clothes,
blankets, flashlights, batteries, and medical supplies on
hand. And most importantly: Have an escape plan. That
way you'll know what to do if a horde of zombies comes
stumbling down your street looking for *braaaaaains!*

THE CENTERS FOR ZOMBIE CONTROL
The Centers for Disease Control (CDC) is a U.S.
government agency that protects the public in the event

of a disease outbreak. Not surprisingly, when the CDC printed up a "Zombie Preparedness Guide" in 2011, people freaked. A CDC official quickly reassured the public—"There has never been a single substantiated report of a real zombie." But the official did not rule out the possibility of the dead rising to feast on the living. What's the CDC's plan for dealing with an undead outbreak? Here's an excerpt from the "Zombie Preparedness Guide":

> If zombies did start roaming the streets, CDC would conduct an investigation much like any other disease outbreak. CDC would provide technical assistance to cities, states, or other nations dealing with a zombie infestation. This assistance might include consultation, lab testing and analysis, patient management and care, tracking of contacts, and infection control.

Hopefully, the doctors at the CDC never have to save us from a zombie attack. But just in case, Uncle John has a survival plan, too: *RUN!*

•　•　•

TONGUELESS TWISTERS

For zombies and others who mostly speak in vowels.

Eater Iper icked an eck of ickled eppers.

Izzy Izard i-i-iz an izard, iz ee?

Air's oo oots are ooties.

Ix ows in an arn, en igs in an ig en.

FASHION FAILS

. . . .

*Bell-bottoms. The mullet. Jeggings. All bad ideas, and yet
not nearly as bad as what these stars call fashion!*

GAG-A

Lady Gaga has referred to her style as "commentary
on what it means to be a lady." Somehow, that just
doesn't explain the meat dress she wore for the 2010
MTV Video Music Awards. A creation of designer Franc
Fernandez, Gaga's body-hugging dress was made entirely
of raw meat. So were the matching hat, shoes, and purse.
"After time spent under the lights, it would smell like
the rotting flesh it is and likely be crawling in maggots,"
said a spokesperson for PETA (People for the Ethical
Treatment of Animals).

ELTON'S JUST DUCKY

In 1975, Elton John wore a Donald Duck suit at a live
performance in New York City's Central Park. Why? "It
just made me laugh," said the singer. He wasn't laughing
for long. Turns out a duck suit is a bit…impractical in
performance. "When I tried to sit down, the costume's
bum was so big that it tipped me forward," said Elton.
"My nose was practically pitched onto the keyboard."

KATY-GO-ROUND

Over the years, pop star Katy Perry has dressed up as a Christmas tree, a fruit bowl, a snowman (snow-woman?), and a movie ticket. But the dress she wore to the 2008 MTV Europe Music Awards really had heads spinning. The dress's short skirt looked exactly like a colorful circus carousel. Exotic animals sparkling with Swarovski crystals circled around it. Best of all: The carousel actually rotated! "The inside of the skirt is full of bearings, nuts, and fittings to make the rotation possible," said designer Manish Arora. Unfortunately, it didn't have a motor, so Katy had to keep reaching down to spin the carousel herself.

RAPPED TO FAIL

The *Huffington Post* described the outfit rapper Nicki Minaj wore to the 2011 MTV Video Music Awards like this: "Nicki went to Toys "R" Us, gathered up all the brightly colored toys she could find, affixed them to her body, and then topped off the look with hair and jewelry inspired by tasty desserts." The rapper's outfit included a life-size ice-cream-cone necklace, a cartoon-print face-mask, and something that looked like the head of a platypus stuck to the top of her right foot. As for the hair? Imagine a neon yellow-and-pink cinnamon bun stuck to the top of someone's head. Yep. That's pretty much what it looked like. As one blogger put it, "Nicki's VMA getup is the epitome of epic fail."

CANINE
CORPSE PATROL

....

When the FBI can't find a body, they call in the big dogs.

BOMB SNIFFING DOGS can smell materials used to make explosives. Drug sniffing dogs can sniff out marijuana stashed in a school locker. Human Remains Detection Canines, or HRD dogs, are trained to the recognize...the smell of death. And they do it with amazing accuracy: a trained dog can detect the scent of a dead body on the ground, even if it was removed from the spot a *year* earlier.

HRD training starts with "fresh scent sources." (Yes, it's as icky as it sounds.) Dogs learn to sniff out hair, bone, teeth, tissue, blood, and other body fluids, but not from live humans—only from corpses. By the end of training HRD dogs can find bodies both above and below ground. They can even tell if a body has been dumped in a lake. How? By sniffing the water's surface for tiny gas bubbles seeping from a corpse rotting underwater.

The FBI usually calls in HRD dogs to find a specific missing person. If that person is a murder victim, finding the body is a crucial step in solving the crime. Thanks to HRD dogs, the FBI "nose" where to look!

KICK THE
SEVERED HAND

· · · · · · · · · · · · · · · · · · · ·

*A careless student has cut off a hand in shop class.
What's a teacher to do? Lead a game of kick-the-hand!*

WHAT YOU NEED: old glove, newspaper, red spray paint
HOW TO PLAY:

1. Stuff the glove with newspaper. Spray-paint it with "blood drops" and let it dry.

2. Put the severed hand in the center of the playing area. The "shop teacher" guards the hand, closes his eyes, and counts to 50 while the "students" hide.

3. Then the teacher looks for the hiders. When the teacher sees a student, he calls out, "I see you, Jake!"

4. The teacher and the student race to see who kicks the severed hand first. If the teacher kicks it, Jake is out and joins the group in "after-school detention." If Jake kicks it, he joins the "school's out" group.

5. The game continues until the teacher has found all the hiders and the last person has kicked the hand.

6. If the detention group is bigger, the teacher wins. If the school's-out group is bigger, the students win.

Black and White Party

by Valeri Gorbachev

One day Frankenstein, Mummy, and Witch saw a poster for a party.

HOLEY FLORIDA!

. . . .

Talk about pulling the rug out from under your feet.

THE WINTER PARK SINKHOLE
At 7:00 p.m. on May 8, 1981, a tree was suddenly sucked into the ground in Winter Park, Florida. Strange. But not nearly as strange as what happened 10 hours later: a sinkhole appeared under a public swimming pool. It grew rapidly to about 335 feet wide and 110 feet deep. It swallowed the pool, a two-story house, two streets, six commercial buildings, and five Porsches at a car dealership. Miraculously, nobody died.

WHAT'S GOING ON: The earth may look solid, but don't be fooled, especially when the stone beneath the ground is limestone as it is in Winter Park. All it takes to dissolve limestone is wate—and time. Water carves limestone into caves and caverns and passages. In time, it dissolves the roofs and walls of those underground spaces. If the water table is high: no problem. If the water table drops, *wham!* Those weakened walls and roofs collapse. Result: a sinkhole. Ironically, Winter Park's building boom probably caused the sinkhole. As the city pumped water out of the ground and into new homes and businesses, the water table got lower and lower until the roof of an underground cavern collapsed. After the disaster, the city stabilized the sinkhole, sealed it up, and turned it into a lake.

BLOODY MIRACLE

....

Every mad scientist needs to do experiments with blood.
But fake blood leads to fewer arrests. Bwa-ha-ha!

WHAT YOU NEED:
- Metal mixing bowl
- Spoon
- Water
- Red food coloring
- Heavy-duty, quart-sized ziptop bag
- Wooden or metal skewers
- The kitchen sink

WHAT TO DO:
1. First, mix up some blood. Pour a few cups of water into the bowl. Squirt in red food coloring and stir, adding more food coloring until the mix turns blood red.
2. Set the zip-top bag in the sink and fill it with water. Push out as much air as you can, and seal the bag.
3. Here's the scary part: poke a skewer through one side of the bag, into the blood, and out the other side. Keep going to see how many skewers you can poke through without causing the bag to bleed.

DR. JOHNENSTEIN SAYS: The bloody bag doesn't leak because the zip-top bag is made of stretchy elastic molecules that cling to the skewers and form seals at the holes. Also, pushing air out of the bag before closing it reduces air pressure inside it. If you poke a skewer into the airy part of the bag, the blood will spurt—so watch out!

HOWL AT THE MOON

· ·

And now…Uncle John will teach you how to fight off a pack of werewolves. Just kidding. We don't have a clue how to do that. But here's what we do know…

WEREWOLF FACT #1: There is no scientific evidence whatsoever that werewolves exist or have ever existed.

WEREWOLF FACT #2: People report werewolf sightings all over the world and have done so for hundreds of years.

RUNNING WITH THE WEREWOLVES

These days, people who claim to have seen werewolves are often laughed at (or told to buy eyeglasses). But a few hundred years ago, things were different. In France, between A.D. 1520 and 1630, records show that more than 30,000 people either claimed to be werewolves or were accused of being werewolves. Village-wide werewolf hunts were not uncommon. And they often ended violently for the alleged werewolves—much like the Salem Witch Trials of the 1690s.

But werewolf sightings in America? Linda Godfrey, author of the *Real Wolfmen: True Encounters in Modern America*, claims that more than 100 people sent her stories of their experiences with actual werewolves. These "werewolves" aren't the creatures you've seen in movies— humans who shift into werewolf shape beneath the full moon. Godfrey doesn't think they're shape-shifting humans at all. Her research leads her to believe they're "some type of wolf that has adapted to walk bipedally" (upright on two legs). If American werewolves don't look like Jack Nicholson in *Wolf* or Taylor Lautner in *Twilight*, what do they look like? These details from actual sightings show what to watch for when you're watching out for werewolves.

GREGGTON, TEXAS, 1958

On a hot summer night, Mrs. Delburt Gregg pushed her bed close to a bedroom window. A storm was brewing nearby, and she thought the breeze would cool her down so she could sleep. It worked. Mrs. Gregg nodded off. But something woke her up…something scratching at the window screen. Lightning flashed, revealing "a huge, shaggy, wolflike creature" with "bared white fangs." Texas women can be tough—instead of screaming and running, Mrs. Gregg dove for a flashlight. She shone it into the yard just in time to see the creature disappear into a clump of bushes. A short time later, she saw an extremely tall man emerge from the bushes, walk across the yard to the road, and vanish into the darkness.

DELAVAN, WISCONSIN, 1989

Driving home from work late one night, Lorianne Endrizzi saw a creature kneeling by the roadside. It had a wolflike snout, fangs, claws, and pointed ears. The creature was built like "a man who had worked out a little bit." In its paws: a road-killed animal. Endrizzi didn't jump to conclusions. She went to the local library, where she found a drawing of a similar creature—a werewolf.

CEDARVILLE, ILLINOIS, 2002

As a woman and her sixteen-year-old daughter drove across a bridge just before dusk, the car's headlights caught the attention of a creature hunched down on the side of the road. The creature looked up. Its yellow-gold eyes locked with the driver's. "It had dark wiry fur," she said, "and a muzzle. I don't remember a tail." What she did remember: It was crouched on its hind legs and turned its upper body toward the car, like a human would, not just its head, like a wolf would. "If it had stood up, it would have been slightly under six feet tall," said the driver. Her daughter, Angel, described the creature this way: "The best thing I can think of to describe it was the werewolf in *Buffy the Vampire Slayer*." Neither mother nor daughter admitted to being afraid. What Mom did admit? "We don't go walking by ourselves anymore."

• • •

Knock, knock!
Who's there?
A Fred!
A Fred who?
Who's a Fred of the Big Bad Wolf?

IN THE NEWS: DEAD WEIRD

. . . .

More proof that truth is stranger than fiction.

IF YOU'VE EVER WATCHED the TV program, *Storage Wars*, you know that all kinds of strange things can be hidden in storage lockers. U-Storage Manager Kevin McKeon was about to auction the contents of a 10 by 10-foot unit. The renters had not made payments for more than a year. Before the auction, McKeon made one final call. He contacted the original renters' granddaughter, Rebecca Ann Fancher. "You can't sell our stuff!" Rebecca Ann said. "My mother told me on her deathbed that Grandma is in the storage unit."

McKeon was skeptical, so he didn't check the unit until a week later. Inside, he discovered old TVs, trashbags of stored stuff, and a hand-made blue casket that contained the remains of Ann Bunche (Grandma). After he got over the shock, he placed a call to the Clearwater, Florida, police. Further investigation revealed that Grandma had been in the unit since her death—17 years earlier. Seems her daughter, Bobbie Barnett Hancock (also deceased by the time the body was found), "just couldn't part with her." No charges were filed against the surviving family members.

HALLOWEENIES

· · · · · · · · · · · · · · · · · · · ·

These pranksters put the "weenie" into Halloween.

INDUBITABLY, WATSON

One Halloween, North London resident Richard Watson and some friends decided to host a Mad Scientist Party at their building. They dressed up in white lab coats and silly wigs. And they put on a display of showy "experiments" to entertain guests. The party was in full swing when police entered the building for a routine check. Officers took one look at the chemicals scattered around and arrested Watson under Britain's Anti-Terrorism Act.

The entire area was evacuated, and roads were cordoned off with police tape. Watson was searched, handcuffed, and interrogated. "They told me they were arresting me on suspicion of making explosives. I laughed at first, but then I realized they were being serious."

Once the police determined that the suspicious-looking materials were just food coloring, bicarbonate of soda, and vinegar, they released Watson without charges.

MOWED OVER

A man driving along Organ Church Road in Salisbury, North Carolina, was horrified when he spotted a blood-spattered body caught beneath a riding lawn mower. The frantic motorist called 911. "He's laying right underneath

the lawn mower," the caller told 911. "He ain't moving."
Emergency responders got ready to rush to the scene. But
before they left, another 911 call came in: "Don't go!" the
caller said. "It's just a Halloween display."

Seems Salisbury teen Chris Deaton had dressed
a dummy in blue jeans splattered with fake blood. He'd
stuck brown work boots on its feet and work gloves
on its hands. Then he put a beer can in the dummy's
hand to make the scene seem more realistic. (Drinking
and lawnmowing don't mix, kiddies!) No charges were
filed against the original 911 caller or the Halloween
prankster.

KNOCK YOURSELF OUT

If dressing up like a monster and then popping out at
someone sounds like a good idea, think again. In 2012,
two kids were working together on a prank at their
school. One kid dressed like a wolfman wearing a top
hat, then he hid in a trash can beside the soda machine.
Another kid stopped a boy in the hall for a chat to give
the wolfman a chance to pull his prank. They should
have picked a different victim. This kid had lightning-
fast reflexes. When the wolfman popped out of the can,
the boy smacked him in the snout and knocked him
right back into the trash. *Pow!*

•   •   •

Q: What time is it when King Kong sits on your hat?
A: Time to get a new hat.

CHOCOLATE-CHIP COOKIE D'OH

· ·

Itching to get back at people who gobble up the cookie dough and swear it wasn't them? Have we got a recipe for you!

WHAT YOU NEED:

- Colander or sieve
- Paper towels
- Food processor or blender
- Mixing bowl
- Spatula or wooden spoon
- Serving bowl and plate
- 1 can chickpeas
- ⅛ teaspoon salt

- ⅛ teaspoon baking soda
- ½ teaspoon vanilla extract
- ¼ cup rolled oats
- ½ cup chocolate chips
- Fruit slices or graham crackers, for serving

WHAT TO DO:

1. Pour the chickpeas into the colander or sieve. Drain and rinse them, then pat them dry with paper towels. Remove any bits of skin that you see.

2. Put the chickpeas, salt, baking soda, vanilla, and oats into a food processor or blender. Process until the ingredients form a paste about the consistency of smooth peanut butter. (Stop blending and stir the mixture once or twice, if needed.) If the "dough" seems too thin, add a spoonful of flour. If it's too thick, add a spoonful of water.

3. Transfer the dough to a mixing bowl. Use a spatula or a wooden spoon to stir in the chocolate chips.

4. Leave the "cookie dough" out on the counter to see who bites. (And hide nearby with a camera to document the looks on their faces.)

5. If no one takes the bait, scoop a generous amount of the finished dough into a serving bowl and set the bowl on a plate. Surround it with graham crackers or fruit slices and serve it up. (Sssh! Don't tell anyone, but this stuff actually tastes yummy!)

• • •

THAT'S CRAZY!

Healthcare just isn't what it used to be…thank goodness!

AUSTRALIA'S Beechworth Lunatic Asylum opened in 1867. It quickly developed a reputation for admitting patients against their will. All it took to have someone committed was the signature of two doctors. To get out? Eight people had to sign the release form. Once inside, patients had to endure treatments such as the "Darwin chair." A patient would be strapped into the revolving chair. Then doctors would spin the chair so fast that the patient would bleed from the mouth, nose, and ears. The asylum closed in 1995, but not before 3,000 patients had died there.

TEAM SPIRITS

∙∙∙∙∙∙∙∙∙∙∙∙∙∙∙∙∙∙∙∙∙∙

Here's the "Who's Boo!" in the world of sports.

SPORT: Basketball
SPIRIT: Effie the maid
STORY: In 2010, New York Knicks center Eddy
Curry tossed fitfully in his room on the tenth floor of
Oklahoma City's century-old Skirvin Hotel. Visiting
NBA squads often stay at the Skirvin, but it was the
night before a Knicks' game against Oklahoma City, and
Curry couldn't sleep. He was too worried about the hotel
ghost—Effie the maid. Legend says that in the 1930s, the
hotel's owner, W.B. Skirvin, locked Effie in a room to
stop her from creating a scandal that involved the baby
locked in the room with her. When she couldn't escape,
Effie leaped out the window with the baby in her arms.

"They said it happened on the tenth floor, and I'm
the only one staying on the tenth floor," said Curry.

Other hotel guests have reported that Effie roams
the halls at night, slamming doors and causing other
mischief. Then there's the wailing baby guests hear—
when no baby is staying on the premises.

"The place is haunted," said Curry's teammate,
forward Jared Jeffries. "It's scary." So was the Knicks loss
to the Oklahoma Thunder the next day: 106–88.

SPORT: Baseball

SPIRIT: Gettysburg Eddie

STORY: Eddie Plank was the first left-handed pitcher to win 300 Major League baseball games. He retired in 1917 from the St. Louis Browns. His nickname, "Gettysburg Eddie," came from his hometown, Gettysburg, Pennsylvania. Eddie died there on February 24, 1926.

Seventy years later—on February 24, 1996— Gettysburg College professor Peter Stitt was asleep in the house where Plank passed away. He woke to a series of strange sounds. "It was kind of a thunk sound, followed by a softer wush-type sound," said Stitt. Like someone pitching a baseball.

Stitt peeked around the door and saw something "kind of fly across." Then he heard that soft noise, and the thing came back. Stitt had no idea what he was seeing. "I thought I saw some light, wispy things. Very, very odd, like fabric or something, just something there, then…it's gone." The sounds continued for weeks. Then they ended, on March 31. Stitt thought he knew why: Baseball season traditionally begins on April 1. "Eddie was doing his spring training," Stitt said.

SPORT: Football

SPIRIT: Gipp

STORY: Notre Dame football star George Gipp died of pneumonia soon after his final game in 1920. The legend is that he stayed out late one night, and his dormitory was locked when he returned. He fell asleep on the steps of Washington Hall on the university campus, became sick soon after, and then died. Notre Dame students have claimed to see Gipp's ghost in and near Washington Hall over the years. For some reason, he's sometimes riding a white horse.

SPORT: Hockey

SPIRIT: Dorothy Mae

STORY: The Hockey Hall of Fame building in Toronto, Ontario, Canada, used to be a branch office of the Bank of Montreal. One day in 1953, a bank teller named Dorothy Mae Elliott shot herself to death there. She may have been caught stealing money. Or she may have been upset because her boyfriend left her—no one knows for sure. But after Dorothy's death, the building developed some weird ticks that still torment the hockey museum today. Lights flick on and off. Doors and windows open for no reason, and moans and screams are sometimes heard. Some employees report phantom hands touching their shoulders when they work alone at night.

Former Hockey Hall employee Rob Hynes told about a strange feeling that drew him to a dark conference room early one morning. "One of the chairs was turning as if a breeze was in there," Hynes said. "It actually moved right into my hand. I'm rather skeptical about ghosts, but I just freaked out and ran out of there."

A young boy visiting the Hall saw something, too. "Don't you see her, don't you see her?" he yelled. Seems he saw a woman with long black hair "going in and out of the walls."

LOCKED IN

· · · · · · · · · · · · · · · · · · · ·

Sure, you can get in the can—but can you get back out?

THE CAPTAIN OF A CHAUTAUQUA Airlines
flight from North Carolina to New York City decided
to take a bathroom break before landing. But when
he tried to get out of the restroom, the door jammed,
trapping him inside. The pilot pounded on the door until
he got the attention of a passenger, and asked him to alert
the crew. Bad idea. Why? Because the passenger had what
sounded like a Middle Eastern accent.

When the passenger tried to explain through the
cockpit door that the captain was locked in the john, the
copilot thought he might be a terrorist. He radioed this
message to the tower: "The captain disappeared in the
back, and, uh, I have someone with a thick foreign accent
trying to access the cockpit."

Air-traffic controllers advised the flight crew to make
an emergency landing. Fighter jets scrambled just before
the captain fought his way out of the bathroom. "There
is no threat!" he radioed the tower. The FBI showed up
anyway. So did Port Authority cops. In the end, authorities
agreed that the incident was a really weird series of events.

FEAR FACTOR: Delta Airlines allows antlers to be
carried on board, as long as they don't have any flesh still
attached. (Eeuw!)

HANAKO,
THE TOILET GHOST

· · · · · · · · · · · · · · · · · · · ·

On the third floor...in the third stall...she is waiting.

BOO!
In primary schools in Japan, there's a scary legend told in hushed voices: The spirit of a little girl lives in the girls' bathroom on the third floor. The schoolkids call her *Toire no Hanako-san*. In English, that translates to "Hanako of the Toilet." She has pale skin, dark eyes, red lips, and wears a red dress. She looks kind of sweet with her bobbed hair. But don't let that fool you. Hanako-san has a mean streak!

FLUSH OUT THE GHOST

If you're brave, and you want her to appear, you must follow these instructions:

- Go into the third-floor bathroom...alone.
- Slowly walk up to the third stall.
- Knock three times on the stall door: *Knock, knock, knock.*
- Ask out loud, "Are you there, Hanako-san?"
- If she is in the stall, she will reply, "Yes, I am here."
- DO NOT open the door. Just run away. Otherwise, Hanako-san will pull you in and stuff you down the toilet!

WHO WAS SHE?

Kids in Japan have been telling Hanako-san ghost stories since the 1950s. Some believe that she was once a real girl. One day, during World War II, Hanako-san stayed after school and played a game of hide-and-seek with her friends. She decided to hide in the third stall in the third-floor bathroom. While she was alone in there, there was a surprise attack from enemy war planes. A bomb exploded in the bathroom where Hanako-san was hiding. Her body was no more…but some say that her tormented spirit remained.

GRADE-A GHOST

The best way to keep Hanako-san from harming you: Let her be. Unless she is called, she will remain in her toilet lair. But if Hanko-san does try to capture you, there is one thing you can do: Show her a test that you took that you got a good grade on. Then she might leave you alone. Why? Because Hanako-san was a good student herself.

TRUTH OR FICTION?

Is Hanako-san simply an urban legend used to scare schoolkids into behaving better (or asking to use the bathroom less often)? Or is she a real ghost? A few students have actually reported seeing her. And a lot more don't want to take any chances. In fact, some students have been so scared to go to the third-floor bathroom alone that they actually peed their pants!

CHICKEN WINGS

· ·

An Uncle John's Eerily Twisted Tale!

WE WERE CAMPING in the patch of woods behind Scotty's house one night. We'd pitched a tent, but we weren't exactly roughing it. By the time the campfire started dying out, we'd scarfed down bags of candy, bottles of soda, and a huge bucket of chicken wings.

"Let's call it a night." Scotty started to pour water on the coals, but I stopped him.

"It's better to have some light," I said.

"What for?" Scotty asked. "We're going to sleep."

"What if I need to get up at night?" I said.

"Chicken!" Scotty snorted.

"No, I'm not I—"

Just then, the chicken-wing bucket toppled over. Chewed-over chicken bones slid out on the ground.

Scotty stared at the bucket. "Must be the wind."

But there wasn't any wind. The night was hot and humid, and there hadn't been a breeze in days.

Scotty shrugged. "Let's get some sleep," he said. He held the water bottle over the coals.

"Don't," I said.

He laughed again and doused the fire. "Chicken," he said. "*Bwaak, bwaak.*"

It took a while for me to fall asleep. I kept hearing

shuffling sounds outside the tent. Sometime after I nodded off, the tent started shaking. Then the whole thing started sliding along the ground...with us inside.

"What's going on?" Scotty said as he jolted awake.

"How should I know?" I said.

The tent picked up speed, thumping and bumping along the ground. I took an elbow to the nose. Scotty got a knee in the gut. *Oof! Ugh! Smack!* And then—we were falling. Scotty screamed.

"Ouch!" I yelled as we landed in a heap. The tent collapsed on top of us. I scrambled to find the flap and unzip it. Then I looked out and up. We were at the bottom of a deep hole. I could see stars directly above us, but nothing else. And then...a small, hazy, white head peeked over the lip of the hole, gazing down at us.

I gasped. "It's a chicken."

"Don't be ridiculous." Scotty stuck his head out of the tent just as a dozen angry-looking chickens joined the first one, glaring down at us.

"Chickens?" Scotty said. "There aren't any chickens around here."

"There are now. And they're mad."

The walls of the hole were steep, and I wasn't sure we could get out. And if we did climb up, those chickens would probably peck our fingers. I sat down on the bunched-up tent to think. One lone chicken flapped its wings and floated over the hole. I could see right through it. I burped, tasting candy and hot sauce, and that's when I knew. "It's those wings!" I said. "Those are the ghosts of all the dead chickens we ate."

The other birds were peeking over the edge again.

"It's your fault," I said to Scotty.

"How is it my fault?"

"You insulted them," I said. "It's bad enough to be eaten. But you called me a chicken, like that's a bad thing to be."

Scotty frowned and looked at the chickens. They started *bwaak-bwaak-bwaaking* at him.

"Say you're sorry," I demanded.

"I am not saying I'm sorry to a bunch of dead chickens." The bwaaking got louder and the whole flock of chicken ghosts rose into the air. "OK. OK," said Scotty. "I'm sorry! Now, can you get us out of here?"

One by one, the chickens floated to the bottom of the hole. They grabbed the edges of the tent in their ghostly beaks and flapped their ghostly wings, and suddenly we were airborne.

"Thanks!" I said as they dumped us outside the hole. The chickens walked away. We could hear them clucking for a few minutes, and then all was quiet. Scotty picked up the tent. "We need to repitch this," he said.

"No way," I said. "I'm going home."

"Oh, come on," he said. "Don't be a—"

"Don't be a what, Scotty?"

He grinned. "Don't be a scaredy cat."

I let out a sigh and started to help him pitch the tent. And that's when the cats started to yowl....

THE END

AMERICA'S MOST HAUNTED SCHOOLS

. . . .

*Not all students graduate. Some seem to be
stuck in school...for eternity.*

HAUNTED GYMS

- Bobby Haymaker probably thought it was just another
  day shooting hoops and running laps in the Shoals
  High School gym in Shoals, Indiana. What he didn't
  know: it would be his last day in gym class—ever. The
  unlucky young basketball player dropped dead that
  fateful day. Ever since, students have reported hearing
  someone running laps and bouncing a ball, even
  though the gym appeared to be...empty.

- The ghosts of North Dallas High School in Dallas,
  Texas seem to have left the gym and headed for the
  showers. The locker room door creaks open on its own.
  Students sometimes hear strange metallic "tappings"
  in the showers. And one witness reported smelling a
  "terrible stench" when investigating the odd noises.
  (Wait...is this the boys' locker room?)

HAUNTED BATHROOMS

- The boys' bathroom in Quincy Junior High in Quincy,
  Illinois, seems to be "occupied"—permanently. The
  mumbling, footsteps, and sobs students hear are said to

be made by the ghost of a student who killed himself there after being dumped by his girlfriend. (Who says middle school isn't tough?) There's no proof of such a tragedy actually happened, but students claim teachers keep quiet about it. They don't want other heartbroken students to spend eternity in the stalls.

- At Lyon County Elementary School in Eddyville, Kentucky, it's the girls' bathroom that has students spooked. The story goes that a student was murdered there and ever since she's stalked the stalls. Strange knocking sounds have been heard and students have reported glimpses of dark shadows. This bathroom ghost must also like to play with water—the faucets turn on all by themselves.

HAUNTED HALLWAYS

- Larry the Janitor had a very bad day when the boiler blew up in his face at Corriher Lipe Middle School in Landis, North Carolina, in the 1940s. Now he's reported to wander the halls, jiggling his keys. He's not alone in his nighttime walks. Other ghosts have been seen, including apparitions of children darting around the hallway lockers.
- The Civil War Battle of Chickamauga was fought just two miles from where Gordon-Lee High Memorial School in Chickamauga, Georgia, stands today. "Twenty-five thousand people were killed in two days," says Greg Greenshaw, the school's former history teacher and coach. That might explain the ghostly

footsteps said to march up and down the hallways and the lights that mysteriously flicker on and off. The meaning of the town's name adds to the spookiness of this haunted school. Chickamauga means "The River of Death."

HAUNTED PLAYGROUNDS

- The ghost that reportedly haunts the wooded area next to Wahiawa Elementary School in Hawaii isn't your ordinary misty white specter. Witnesses say the "Green Lady" that lurks in the trees is a scaly creature.
- The swing set in the elementary school's playground in Firmat, Argentina, is a popular place—for ghosts, that is. The two swings on either side of the middle one remain still when no one is on them. The middle swing doesn't. It's been seen swinging all on its own for up to *ten days* before stopping. Police have consulted scientists who have ruled out wind and either magnetic or electrical fields. "We believe it is haunted," says teacher Maria de Silva Agustina. "One child called it the Blair Witch Playground."

• • •

"I'm not afraid of death; I just don't want to be there when it happens."

—Woody Allen

REEL SCREAMERS

* * * * * * * * * * * * * * * * * * * *

Who says kids' movies can't give you nightmares?

THE WIZARD OF OZ (1939)

Monkeys can be scary enough in real life, but when monkeys fly…it's nightmare time! In *The Wizard of Oz*, the Wicked Witch of the West sends her squads of flying monkeys out to kidnap Dorothy. They swarm over Dorothy and her friends, the Cowardly Lion, the Tin Man, and the Scarecrow. Then they stomp the stuffings out of poor Scarecrow, snatch Toto the dog, and fly off with Dorothy in their clutches.

BAMBI (1942)

Many viewers believe *Bambi* contains one of the scariest movie moments of all time. About halfway through the film, Bambi and his mom are nibbling on new spring grass that she's found peeking out of the snow. Then Mom's head lifts and her ears go up. "Run!" she tells him. "Don't look back!" Bambi runs faster and faster with his mother right behind him until—*Bam!* We hear a gunshot. And as masters of horror know, what you *don't* see can be a lot scarier than what you *do* see.

WILLY WONKA AND THE CHOCOLATE FACTORY (1971)

Finding a golden ticket and winning a tour of Willy

Wonka's chocolate factory seems like a dream come true. That is, until the mad chocolate maker loads the kids up for a boat ride on his chocolate river. As the boat speeds down a dark tunnel, Wonka starts singing in a creepy voice: "Not a speck of light is showing, so the danger must be growing. Is the grisly reaper mowing? Yes!" A wild-eyed Wonka continues to sing as images such as a giant millipede crawling over a man's face and a chicken's head being chopped off flash along the tunnel walls.

TOY STORY 3 (2010)

"*Toy Story Three* was the creepiest film I have ever taken my children to," said one mom. "We watched the movie in the theater, and even my oldest, at age ten, was crying." Why? Because of the incinerator scene. Woody, Buzz Lightyear, and their friends are tossed into an incinerator where they slide down a mass of debris toward writhing flames. The characters all join hands and close their eyes as firelight sears their terrified faces.

GREMLINS (1984)

It's scary enough when furry little Gizmo gets wet and writhing furballs starting popping off his body. But that's nothing compared to the scene when Mom grabs the butcher knife. She stalks the evil gremlins into the kitchen, shoves one of them into a mixer and turns it on, stabs another one to death, and then pushes a third into the microwave and hits the start button. Result? Gremlin guts explode all over the microwave's glass door.

CURSE OF THE...

· · · · · · · · · · · · · · · · · · · ·

We're not saying curses are real. We have no idea. But if you want to believe, these stories may convince you.

CURSE OF THE... HOPE DIAMOND

The Hope Diamond is one of the most famous jewels in the world, both for its size and its history. The average diamond is about 1 *carat*—the measure of weight used for gems. The Hope Diamond is a whopping 46 carats. Its size is only half the story. The other half earned the gem the nickname "Diamond of Doom." Some say a trader named Jean Baptiste Tavernier started the curse when he stole the giant blue stone from the eye socket of a statue in India. After selling the stone, he went bankrupt. The next owner, Louis XVI, gave the diamond to his wife, Marie Antoinette. Shortly thereafter, they were both beheaded. Subsequent owners have been murdered, committed suicide, or suffered significant financial mishaps. Since 1958, the Smithsonian Institution has held the Hope Diamond, with no additional curse reports...yet.

CURSE OF THE... EGYPTIAN KING

For hundreds of years, Egypt's boy-king Tutankhamen rested undisturbed in an elaborately decorated tomb. In 1922, however, archaeologists discovered the tomb, and the curse of King Tut began. An English earl named

George Herbert had provided financial backing for the expedition. A year after the tomb was opened, Herbert died of blood poisoning. His lead archaeologist, Howard Carter, lost two assistants during the project, and a number of tourists who visited the site fell ill or died after leaving the tomb. One theory suggests that an airborne bacteria or fungus was present in the tomb, but that has never been confirmed. King Tut's mummy continues to tour museums around the world, should you want to test the curse in person.

CURSE OF THE ... ROYAL WEDDING

It's normal for a thing or two to go wrong at weddings. But when Italy's Prince Amedeo I married Maria Vittoria dal Pozzo on May 30, 1867, things way went beyond wrong. From start to finish, six people involved in the wedding died on the royal couple's wedding day. First, the woman who was supposed to set out the wedding dress hung herself instead of the gown. Second, the father-of-the-groom's aide (Dad was King Victor Emmanuel II of Italy) fell off his horse and died. Third, a colonel leading the wedding procession to the church had a sunstroke...and died. Fourth, the palace gatekeeper was found in a pool of blood—his throat had been slit. Fifth: The couple soldiered on and said their vows, after which the best man shot himself in the head. Sixth, the stationmaster was crushed to death beneath the wheels of the honeymoon train. Ten years later, the "curse" claimed victim #7: Princess Maria died after childbirth.

THE CURSE OF ... SUPERMAN

Rumors fly faster than a speeding bullet in Hollywood, including the one about the Man of Steel: Superman. Some say that Superman is "a role to die for." Voice actor Bud Collyer survived two stints as the voice of Superman in cartoons (early 1940s and mid-1960s). But in 1969, when he returned to voice the role for "The Batman Superman Hour," he died of a circulatory problem. George Reeves, who played the superhero in a 1950s TV series, died of a gunshot wound to the head in 1959. Whether he shot himself or was murdered is still a mystery. Christopher Reeve, best known for his Superman role in the '70s and '80s, broke his neck in a horseback riding accident in 1995. Reeve was completely paralyzed and could no longer breathe without the help of a respirator. His Lois Lane co-star—actress Margot Kidder—was partially paralyzed in car crash in 1990 and went on to suffer a nervous breakdown.

THE CURSE OF ... AMEN-RA

A journalist named William Stead was aboard the ill-fated Titanic when it sank on its maiden voyage. Survivors say Stead told a harrowing tale during the journey. He began the tale at dinner on the night of April 12, 1912. It was about an Egyptian princess named Amen-Ra...or, more accurately, her mummy. Stead claimed to have first seen the mummy at the British Museum. Wherever this mummy was stored—Stead swore—disaster followed. A worker who lifted her coffin fell and broke his leg. A museum guard dropped dead at his desk. A photographer who snapped a photo of the mummy went home and shot himself. And, Stead claimed, Amen-Ra's mummy was now aboard...the Titanic. Stead finished his creepy tale just after midnight on April 13. On April 15, the journalist and 1,516 others went down with the ship, but what about the mummy? No one knows. It wasn't listed as cargo on the ship's manifest. And, what Stead saw at the British Museum wasn't actually a mummy. It was a mummy *case* which has been on display there since 1890. Scholars say that the mummy that was once inside the case probably never left Egypt at all. (Or did it?)

• • •

WRETCHED RIDDLES

Q: What do you call a ghost with a broken leg?
A: A hoblin' goblin.

Q: What did the mummy say to the detective?
A: Let's wrap this case up.

Q: What happened when the Wolfman swallowed a watch?
A: He got ticks.

Q: What do you get when you cross Bambi with a ghost?
A: Bam*boo!*

DR. PUKE

· ·

Would you drink vomit to make a point? This guy did!

FFIRTH IN MEDICINE

In the late 1700s, Stubbins Ffirth was a medical student at the University of Pennsylvania in Philadelphia. He had witnessed the deadly yellow fever epidemic of 1793 when 10 percent of the residents of his city had died, and he wanted to find out how it had spread.

Yellow fever was a horrible disease. It started with fever and headaches. Next came chills and vomiting. Then the victim's skin turned yellow. That was followed by "black vomit," delirium, coma, and...death.

At the time, doctors had just begun to explore "germ theory." The theory said that microscopic entities could spread from person to person through bodily fluids such as vomit, sweat, urine, or blood. Ffirth thought that was hokum. In his opinion, yellow fever was caused by the heat and noise of Philadelphia summers. After all, the disease was rare in winter.

FFIRTH IN THE OLD HEAVE-HO

Ffirth set out to disprove germ theory by feeding fresh vomit from yellow-fever patients to birds, cats, and dogs. They didn't get sick. Ffirth wanted to continue his experiments on people, but (strangely enough) no one stepped forward for exposure to the deadly fever. So Ffirth turned himself into a medical guinea pig. His goal: to prove that no matter how often he exposed himself to the disease, he would not catch it.

Ffirth wrote that he deliberately "took the breath of my patients in my face." Then he collected fresh vomit from victims and spread it on his skin. He put some puke in his eye and then heated some up in a pan and inhaled the fumes. Next he took several hearty drinks of his patients' vomit.

Of course, other bodily fluids had to be tested as well. So Ffirth did the same things with his patients' blood, saliva, sweat, and urine. When none of this made him sick, he declared that germ theory was "nothing more than pseudoscientific claptrap."

FFIRTH IN BEING WRONG

Ffirth's experiments caused scientists to look for another reason for the spread of yellow fever. That's too bad, because yellow fever is extremely contagious. But it must be transmitted directly into the blood stream. It wasn't until a century later that a Cuban scientist named Carlos Finlay showed that the disease was spread mostly by the bites of mosquitoes. (Which also explained why it was most common in the summer.)

So why didn't Stubbins Ffirth catch the disease and croak? It seems that the fluids he used came from late-stage patients who were no longer contagious.

• • •

TRI-STATE TWISTER

....

Here's the story of one of the most terrifying storms in U.S. history.

PANIC ATTACK

It started without warning on March 18, 1925, around 1:01 p.m. No storms had been predicted. At the time, weather forecasters weren't even allowed to use the word "tornado." The word had been banned in 1887, when the U.S. Army Signal Corps forecasted the country's weather. Tornadoes were too unpredictable, the Corps reasoned. If you couldn't tell where they might touch down, why send people into a panic?

When trees started snapping north-northwest of Ellington, Missouri, no one was prepared for what was to come. A funnel touched down three miles outside of town, killed a farmer, and then moved to the northeast at speeds between 62 and 73 mph. This was no ordinary tornado. It was a mile-wide monster with winds churning at speeds up to 300 mph. It would rage for 3½ hours and plow through three states: Missouri, Illinois, and Indiana. And it would leave a path of destruction 234 miles long.

TODDLING TOWARD OZ

Wallace Akin spent his career as a tornado scientist at Drake University in Iowa. In 1925, Akin was 2 years old.

He lived with his family in Murphysboro, Illinois. Akin shared his memories of that terrifying day in his 1992 history of the Tri-State Tornado, *The Forgotten Storm*. It may read like *The Wizard of Oz*, but it's real.

An invading army of debris swept over the western hill—trees, boards, fences, roofs. Day became night. The house began to levitate and, at the same time, the piano shot across the room, gouging the floor and carpet where I had played only moments before. The walls began to crack as the roof ripped free and disappeared, joining the swirling mass of debris. But the walls and floor held as we and the house took flight.

GHOST TOWN

By the time the tornado spun out of Murphysboro, it had left the largest weather-related death toll within a single U.S. city in history: 234. The deaths included at least 25 students crushed under falling walls in three schools. But the twister had another 2 hours and 130 miles to go before it petered out.

In all, 19 separate communities were affected. Two towns were wiped off the map: Gorham, Illinois, and Griffin, Indiana. Two others experienced 90 percent destruction: Annapolis, Missouri, and Parrish, Illinois. An estimated total of 15,000 homes were demolished, 695 people died, and 2,027 were injured. Parrish was never rebuilt—it became a tornadic ghost town.

• • •

SOMETHING WICKED

· · · · · · · · · · · · · · · · · · · ·

An Uncle John's Eerily Twisted Tale.

A **RAW WIND BIT** into the back of my neck as I hurried home after football practice. I shivered, but not because of the wicked wind. Because I'd made a really stupid promise to the team. We were trying to raise money for new football jerseys. And when Coach asked for suggestions, that cold wind sort of blew in one of my ears and out the other taking my brain with it. That was the only reason I could think of for the lame idea that popped out of my mouth.

"Let's have a kissing booth at the Halloween Carnival!"

After the hoots and catcalls and kissy noises had died down, Coach had said, "Any other ideas?"

That's when Scot Turdle, the fullback who loved nothing more than sacking me in every practice, hooted, "Yo, Bradbury! Better keep that twin sister of yours out of the booth. Nobody'd pay to kiss her!"

And that's when Terry Wildman said, "I would!"

And Mike Mitchell said, "Me, too!"

And pretty soon all the guys were saying, "Heck yeah!" and "I'd kiss her twice!" and I got caught up in the excitement and said, "Yeah, so would I!" And then I felt my ears burning like a bonfire and stuttered around for a minute trying to explain that I meant, you know, Rae was kind of cute for a girl, even if she was my twin, so I'd kiss her if she wasn't my twin, but she was, so no—no I wouldn't. *Bleck!* And then I'd spit on the ground like I'd kissed a rotten cabbage or something.

"Good." Coach had slapped his hands together. "So now we know lots of guys would pay to kiss Rae, with the notable exceptions of Scot and Brad. Let's do this thing! Brad," Coach turned to me, "you get the girl, the rest of us will build the booth."

And that's the moment I realized I was in serious trouble. Because no way was Rae gonna volunteer to kiss a bunch of football jerks or anyone else for that matter, especially not if I was the one asking her to do it. Why couldn't I have kept my big mouth shut for once?

"So, I was wondering…"

"No," said Rae.

"But I haven't even—"

"I already know about your stupid kissing booth. Shakira called, and you can count me out." Rae looked up from her iPad and I glanced at the Tweet she was writing: JUST SAY NO TO LAME KISSING BOOTHS! It wouldn't be the Tweet that went 'round the world, but Rae had a lot of followers. So it would go out to pretty much every girl in Jackson Middle School.

"Wait! No!" My shoulders sagged as she clicked SEND. "Why?" I whined.

"Are you kidding? Kissing booths went out with Poodle skirts and penny loafers."

I had no idea what a Poodle skirt or a penny loafer was. But I knew one thing: if Rae didn't volunteer for the booth, Turdle would pound me for it from now till the last football practice of our senior year.

So…here's the thing: If you thought the kissing booth idea was lame, you might think my next idea was lamer. But to me, it was a no-brainer—in a good way, not in a brainless way. After all, Rae wasn't just my twin: She was my *identical* twin. With a few borrowed clothes and some makeup tricks from *Teen Glam* magazine, *bam!* Rae Bradbury would be sitting in the kissing booth on Halloween night as promised.

That wicked October wind was still blowing on Halloween night. It wrapped around my ankles, crept up my knees, and poofed up my Tulle skirt. I slapped it down. How did girls have the nerve to wear clothes that could blow up over their knickers at any minute? It was terrifying—and cold! My teeth were chattering before I was halfway to the field at the edge of town where the carnival was being held. I'd turned my ankle twice in the high-heeled sandals I'd borrowed, and now I was doing this kind of shambling zombie walk instead of the Marilyn Monroe wiggle I'd started out with. It took awhile, but eventually I saw carnival lights winking in the distance and heard eerie music drifting through the trees. The wind blew harder, making branches jangle like skeletons and leaves rattle like loose finger bones.

Somehow, I made it to the booth and limped inside. The guys had decorated it with stuff borrowed from moms and sisters: bright silk pillows, beaded lamps, and so many scented candles my head started to pound. And then…I realized that the pounding wasn't in my head. It was my first customer, pounding on the counter to get my attention. "Yo, Rae!"

My hands went cold and clammy. It couldn't be. I turned so slowly you could hear every vertebrae in my spine click. And there he stood: Scot Turdle—the guy who said no one would pay to kiss my twin—waving a dollar bill and grinning wickedly. I took a deep breath and did the only thing I could do: I puckered up.

Scot planted a big wet one on my lips, then stepped back, grinning even bigger. Then I heard footsteps, and a gasp, and I looked up to see Rae staring back at me. Half the football team seemed to have followed her to the booth, and they all stood behind her with their mouths gaping open. "Uh…hi, Sis." I waved. "Guys."

Turdle turned around and spotted Rae. He looked back at me, and then all the color drained from his face. "EEEE!!" Turdle screamed—I swear—just like a little girl. Then he started rubbing the back of his hand across his mouth and gagging.

Rae gave me a killer grin and a thumbs up. "Well, boys," she said, "since Brad here is obviously a terrible kisser, I'd better take over." And she did…and that's how we raised enough money for new football jerseys. As for Scot Turdle? He ran for the woods that night and was never seen at Jackson Middle School again.

THE END

MEDIEVAL FOOTBALL

. . . .

Who knew the Middle Ages could be this much fun?

IT WASN'T ALL GRUEL AND GRIME in the Middle Ages. Games were afoot then, just as they are now. There was even a medieval version of football, a highly competitive game played between neighboring villages. There was no limit to the number of players. And the game had just one rule: Try to get the "ball" (usually an inflated pig's bladder) past markers on either end of the town in which the game was being played. It was a rough sport. There were so many injuries (and deaths) that, in 1349, Britain's King Edward III tried to have the game banned. Players refused to give it up.

How violent was folk football? The first "balls" used in this game were severed heads tossed into a crowd after an execution. There was also a Scottish verse that warned of the dangers of playing:

Bruised muscles and broken bones,
Discordant strife and futile blows,
Lamed in old age, then cripled withal:
These are the beauties of foot-ball.

FOOTBALL FOOTNOTE: Early footballs weren't made from a pig's skin. They were made from a pig's bladder. A bladder is a hollow organ. It usually holds, well, pee.

WATCH OUT
FOR BARRY!

. . . .

An Uncle John's Eerily Twisted Tale!

NO ONE COULD REMEMBER who'd had the bright
idea to sneak out of camp and hike to the haunted
ravine. But everyone remembered why they'd never do
something so stupid again. It all started when Eddie's
little brother needed to take a leak.

"Where do you think you're going?" Eddie
mumbled when Jake opened the tent flap.

"Outside," said Jake.

"Are you nuts?" Eddie asked. "It's pitch black out there."

"But I have to go."

"Can't you hold it until morning?"

Jake shook his head. "I won't go far."

Eddie propped up on his elbows and turned on his
flashlight. "Take this," he said. "And watch out for Barry."

They were high up in the Adirondack Mountains
for a week of roughing it at scout camp. Last night
someone had pulled out that old legend about the boy
who had wandered away from camp and fallen into a
ravine. He'd screamed for his big brother Barry to rescue
him, but no one heard his cries. By the time they found
him, it was too late. The story always ended with a

warning: "His ghost is still out there, just waiting to pull you into the ravine with him."

Jake figured the story was just something the older kids used to scare the younger ones. As he walked away from the campsite, the wind rustled the leaves in the trees, drowning out the other forest sounds. But then... he did hear another sound: a shrill soft voice calling, "Bah-reeeeee."

Barry? The voice sent a chill through Jake. No way could that story be true. Could it? There was only one way to find out. He would follow the sound. Seeing a ghost would be awesome. Jake walked several yards, then listened again. He heard the voice calling, "Bah-reee!"

Carefully, Jake picked his way through the trees. Within a minute he was standing by the ravine. And the voice sounded close. Very close.

"Bah-reee. Bah-reee."

Jake took one more step.

"Bah-reee. Bah-reee."

He leaned forward, pointing his flashlight into the darkness below. Suddenly, the ground gave way and Jake was falling. "Eddie!" He screamed for his brother all the way down. Luckily for Jake, it had been a rainy spring. He landed with a splash in a vernal pool at the bottom of the ravine. It was deep enough to cushion his fall.

"Bah-ree! Bah-ree!"

Jake jumped. The voice was right beside him now. He poked around in the muddy pool. Where was his flashlight? "Bah-ree. Bah-ree." His knuckles hit metal and he fumbled for the light. "Bah-ree. Bah-ree." Jake's hand shook as he swept the light around the ravine until he spotted a tiny movement.

"Bah-ree. Bah-ree."

Jake laughed. The ghost wasn't a ghost at all. It was a little gray treefrog. He had solved the legend of the haunted ravine.

It took awhile, but Jake managed to climb out of the ravine. Then, just as he reached the top, a hand grabbed his shirt. The ghost! "Leggo!" he yelped, but the hand tugged harder, hauling him up to the top.

"Are you nuts? Stop fighting!" said a familiar voice.

Jake gulped down his terror. "Eddie?"

Eddie and the others had heard his terrified screams echoing off the walls of the ravine and come to the rescue. As the boys hiked back to camp, they peppered Jake with questions: "Did you see the ghost?" "Did it trick you into falling?" "Were you freaked?"

"Yes," Jake answered truthfully, hiding a grin.

That was ten years ago. Scouts still hike to the haunted ravine and pitch a tent for a spooky night in the forest. But if they have to go, they do their best to hold it in.

THE END

FEAR FOOTNOTE: Eastern gray treefrogs are hard to see. They're just an inch or two long. They can change color like a chameleon, going from gray to green to brown to hide themselves. They're only active at night. And they do make a short high-pitched trill sounds a bit like "Barry."

MORE
TERRIBLE TYRANTS

· ·

*On page 81, we told you about some of the most rotten
tyrants in history. These guys were just as bad,
so how could we leave them out?*

TYRANT: Hernan Cortés
WHERE AND WHEN: Spain (A.D. 1485–1547)
THE TERRIBLE DEEDS: Starting with a small army
of Spanish soldiers, this conquistador wiped out three-
quarters of the Aztec population in the area that is now
Mexico and Central America. And that caused the fall of
the Aztec Empire. How did he do it? With weapons these
native people had never seen before: guns, crossbows,
armor, cannons, steel swords, horses, military attack dogs,
and smallpox. At first the smallpox was an accident, but
when Cortés saw how effective a killer the disease could
be, he spread smallpox germs on purpose. Then he sank
his own ships so his men couldn't run away.
WHY DID HE DO IT? Cortés wanted gold and power—
and Montezuma, the Aztec ruler, had plenty of both.
THE TYRANT'S DOWNFALL: The Spanish
government felt Cortés was getting too powerful, so they
called him back to Spain. He was never able to regain the
power he had in Mexico and died a bitter old man.

TYRANT: Countess Elizabeth Bathory, "The Blood Countess"

WHERE AND WHEN: Hungary (A.D. 1560–1614)

THE TERRIBLE DEEDS: The Countess tortured and murdered more than 650 young girls from her region. In the winter, she made them stand naked in the snow and poured cold water over them till they froze. In summer, she covered them with honey till they were killed by insect bites. Then she took a bath in their blood.

WHY DID SHE DO IT? The Countess believed the blood of young girls would keep her young and beautiful.

THE TYRANT'S DOWNFALL: When the Countess tired of torturing peasant girls and servants, she branched out to noble women. That made the upper class finally sit up and take notice. The detailed journal she kept describing her murders proved her guilt. Countess Bathory was sentenced to live alone in a tiny, windowless room in her castle for the rest of her life.

TYRANT: King Leopold II, "The Butcher of Congo"

WHERE AND WHEN: Belgium (A.D. 1835–1909)

THE TERRIBLE DEEDS: This Belgian king became the ruler of the Congo Free State in Africa by pretending to rescue the Congolese people from Arab slavers. Instead, he turned the entire country into a forced labor camp for harvesting rubber. Villages had to provide a certain amount of rubber, and if they didn't, villagers' hands would be lopped off. It's estimated that between 5 and 15 million Congolese were murdered during this tyrant's reign…but he never saw a drop of the blood spilled in his name. In the 23 years he controlled it, Leopold never set foot in the Congo.

WHY DID HE DO IT? Leopold II wanted his tiny country to become a colonial power like England or France. Belgium wasn't interested. So Leopold went private. He equipped an army of 19,000 men (black soldiers with white officers) with rifles, cannons, and machine guns, and sent them against Africans armed mostly with spears. Once the Congo was under his control, he murdered, tortured, and enslaved the Congolese so that he could stuff his pockets with money.

THE TYRANT'S DOWNFALL: In the 1900s, pictures of handless children and rivers choked with bodies in the Congo spread to the outside world. The public outcry started the modern human rights movement. In 1908, the Belgian state forced Leopold to turn over his private ownership of the Congo to his country. He kept the furnaces near his palace burning for eight days straight turning the Congo state records to ash. "I will give them my Congo," Leopold said, "but they have no right to know what I did there." When the tyrant died, his own subjects booed his funeral procession.

•　　•　　•

"There are wrongs which even the grave does not bury."
—**Harriet Ann Jacobs, African-American writer**

A FATE WORSE
THAN DEATH

....

Victorians did everything they could to avoid vivisepulture.
What's that? Being buried alive.

THE BURIED BARON

Most people are afraid of dying. It's human nature.
But during the Victorian era (roughly 1837 until Queen
Victoria's death in 1901), fear turned to panic after a few
people were reportedly buried alive.

The *Thesaurus of Horror* ran a story about a young
Bavarian baron who had been buried in a mausoleum
after a sudden unexplained death. Two days later, the
story said, cemetery workers entered the crypt and found
the baron's body just inside the door. He had apparently
been buried alive and escaped his coffin only to find
himself sealed inside the burial chamber.

In 1877, a British medical journal reported on a
woman who had been declared dead. Three days after
her burial, the crypt she'd been placed in was reopened.
The woman was found with her clothes torn to pieces.
"She had broken her limbs in attempting to extricate
herself from the living tomb," the journal reported.

Victorian readers gobbled up these gruesome tales,
but it wasn't long before intrigue turned to terror. The
public couldn't help but wonder: Who would be next?

INEXACT SCIENCE

Victorians believed death was always preceded by a "death trance": a state of deep unconsciousness in which all signs of life (things like breathing and muscle reflexes) ceased. This state was so similar to death itself that even trained physicians found it nearly impossible to tell the difference. But there was hope. Doctors thought it possible to revive a patient from a death trance. How? Through vigorous—even brutal—resuscitation techniques.

Milder methods of reviving a patient included rubbing the gums with garlic and irritating the nostrils with onion juice or horseradish (today's smelling salts work on the same principal, but use ammonia). One physician relied on "hideous shrieks and excessive noises" to shock the ears. Another preferred jamming a sharpened pencil up the patient's nose.

If these methods didn't wake the patient from the death trance, more gruesome measures were in store. The soles of the feet might be sliced with razor blades or needles stabbed beneath the nail of the big toe. Boiling wax might be poured on the forehead or into the ear canal. In extreme cases, a red-hot poker might be—to put it delicately—"introduced to the corpse's backside."

BEDS FOR THE DEAD

Even after trying such extreme wake-up calls, doctors were still reluctant to pronounce someone dead. The only surefire proof of death? Putrefaction. That's right. In those days, to prove someone was dead, you had to wait for the body to rot. But who wants to keep a rotting corpse around the house? Not only do corpses smell terrible, they pose health risks for the living. The solution: a "waiting mortuary"—a kind of hospital for the dead.

Bodies were kept in warm comfy beds. Each corpse-in-waiting had a ring tied to a string placed on its finger. This string was attached to an alarm system that would be triggered by the slightest movement. Attendants made hourly rounds to check on "patients." Bodies were kept until they either revived...or putrefaction set in.

KEY TO THE AFTERLIFE

Those horrified by the concept of waiting mortuaries (and who had plenty of money) opted for "security coffins" instead. The first recorded security coffin was built for Duke Ferdinand of Brunswick in 1792. It had a window to let in light and a ventilation hole to let in fresh air. Instead of being nailed shut, the lid housed a locking mechanism. The Duke was buried with a set of keys in a special pocket in his burial shroud. One key unlocked the lid and another unlocked the door of his crypt. Despite being buried in the Rolls Royce of security coffins, the Duke stayed dead.

• • •

"All I desire for my own burial is not to be buried alive."
—Lord Chesterfield, 1769

One day, the two nice sisters skipped down to the Nasty River. On the far side of town, the river was sparkling clean. But once it reached the nice sisters' cottage it was...

nasty.

Because the sisters were so nice, they noticed nice things, even in the Nasty River.

Look! A kitten!

He's so cute!

Can we have him?

Only if you are very bad.

We can be bad.

We'll have to break the rules.

Maybe just the little ones?

THE GRIMY TRUTH

. . . .

Great-Grandma Uncle John made the kids bathe every
Saturday, whether they needed to or not. Maybe
she knew something modern moms don't!

SORRY, MOM!

Medical researchers have something to say about
taking daily showers. Don't do it! Why? The outer layer
of skin (called the *horny layer*) is made up of hardened
dead skin cells. Those cells are held together by lipids—
fatty compounds that keep skin moist. Soap and hot
water dissolve those lipids, and scrubbing sends skin's
protective outer layer down the drain. The more showers
you take, the more skin damage. The result? Dry, itchy,
cracked skin. To protect your skin…skip a few showers
every week.

THE CLOTHES SHOWER

Water is tough to come by in space. So volunteers spent
time in a spacecraft cabin simulator to find out what
would happen if they *didn't* bathe. They stayed in the
simulator for weeks. When they came out, researchers
put their clothes in a tub of water. They stood the
volunteers in another tub of water and sprayed them
down. Next, they compared the water in each tub.
About 90 percent of the "crud" was in the clothes water.

Here's why: Clothing absorbs the grease and the *scurf*—scaly or shredded skin—and leaves the skin fairly clean. That means changing clothes in space would be like taking a waterless "clothing shower." The experiment taught volunteers something else: If you don't change your underwear after a few weeks, it starts to dissolve!

STOP SCRUBBING!

If you're human, at this very moment trillions of tiny single-celled creatures called *bacteria* live inside your body. In fact, your body is home to ten times more bacterial cells than human cells. (*Eek!*) As for your skin…it's covered with bacteria!

"The skin is home to a virtual zoo of bacteria," says microbiology professor Martin J. Blaser. At least 182 different kinds of bacteria live in that zoo. But don't rush out and buy antibacterial soap. Although some bacteria are bad for us, most are either harmless or helpful.

Research shows that *good* bacteria on the skin play a big role in keeping out the *bad* bacteria. But antibacterial soap isn't choosy. It kills the good bacteria along with the bad. And that leaves room for deadly bacteria to move in and colonize the body.

LET THEM EAT DIRT

American kids are getting allergies and asthma in record numbers. Medical researchers say it's because they're too clean. (Huh?) That's right. American parents are so hung up on avoiding germs, they keep their homes and their kids too clean. "We've increased our efforts to protect our children from dirt and germs," says allergy specialist Marc McMorris. The result? "The immune system does not have as much to do as it did fifty years ago." With fewer germs to fight off, the body starts fighting other "foreign" things—pollen, mold, animal dander, dust and dust mites, insect stings, and even foods. That fight can cause allergic reactions and even asthma.

Turns out, one of the best way to protect yourself from germs is to go outside and play. Hang out with your friends. Make mud pies. "Don't worry about coming into contact with dirt and germs," says McMorris. Kids exposed to germs at an early age are often healthier than those who stay superclean.

THE EXCEPTION PROVES THE RULE

Don't stop scrubbing your *hands*. Doctors still say that hand washing is the most important thing you can do to stay healthy. Especially…
* before and after touching food,
* after using the bathroom,
* after blowing your nose or coughing,
* after touching pets or other animals, and
* before and after visiting a sick relative or friend.

• • •

FEAR FACTor: As of 2001, the usable body parts of an adult human were worth $46,000,000.

ZOMBIE-RELLA

· · · · · · · · · · · · · · · · · · · ·

An Uncle John's Totally Twisted Tale

ONCE UPON A TIME in a land far away, a beautiful
maiden named Ella lived with her stepmother and
two stepsisters in a beautiful mansion on top of a hill,
next to a radioactive testing facility. Ella was a kind girl
who spent all of her free time caring for the animals
that lived on the mansion's grounds. Her stepmother,
Mildred, and her two stepsisters, Helga and Ingrid, were
lazy, spoiled, and jealous of Ella. They forced her to do
the cooking, the cleaning, the stepsisters' homework, and
the stepmother's taxes, while they lay on the couch and
watched *Keeping up with the Kardashians*.

One day, while Ella was throwing out her stepsisters'
toenail clippings, she saw a racoon climb over the fence
from the testing facility. As it limped toward her, she
noticed that it was missing the top of its skull. "You poor
thing!" said Ella, "let me take care of you!"

When she reached out her hand, the raccoon bit it,
and by the next day, Ella had become a zombie. But even
with her new "walking undead" status—and difficulty
in keeping her legs and arms attached to her body—Ella
was still the most beautiful girl in the kingdom.

One day, as Ella stumbled about the house dusting,
there was a knock at the door. A man in a crimson cape

handed her a scroll tied with a gold ribbon. "The Prince is having a ball to find himself a wife," she read aloud, "and has invited all eligible young ladies in the kingdom to attend."

"A BALL!!!" screeched Helga. "Give me that!" She ripped the scroll from Ella, taking one of her hands with it.

"Ella!" ordered Ingrid. "Reattach that hand and start making my dress at once!"

"Sew all of our dresses!" Ella's stepmother shoved her toward the sewing room (knocking out one of her eyes in the process). "I just know one of my daughters will become a princess by the end of the night!"

Ella popped her eyeball back into its socket and murmured, "I hope it's me!"

"Oh, dear, no! You can't go," Mildred said. "You're a zombie."

"Yeah, you're Zombie-rella!" taunted Ingrid. And they all laughed, which of course made Ella feel terrible.

On the night of the ball, after her stepmother and sisters had left, Ella sat in the yard sewing her hand back on. "I'd give anything to go to the ball," she said with a sigh.

"How about an arm and a leg?" a voice asked from above her.

Ella looked up and gasped. A red-headed woman in a white lab coat, black gloves, and goggles was hovering above her in a jetpack. "Who are you?" asked Ella.

"Call me Professor Godmother," the woman said, floating to the ground in front of Ella. "I'm from the lab next door."

"You scared me," Ella said, staring at the strange little woman.

"That's me—one scary Godmother!" The professor snorted. "And I'm here to help you." She whipped a small bottle from her pocket. "I can use this new molecule-binding glue to put you back together so you can go to that Prince's ball! And, with a little radioactive material, I can also cause a chemical reaction that will turn those rags you're wearing into a shimmering ball gown!"

"You'd do all that for me?" Ella gasped.

The woman raised her goggles to the top of her head. "But of course. We owe it to you, after that whole escaped raccoon, one bite and instant zombie business."

In no time, the transformation was complete and Ella looked stunning. Now all they had to do was get her to the ball.

"Take my jetpack," said Professor Godmother, strapping it over Ella's shoulders. "But remember! You absolutely must leave before midnight. The time-release glue will stop working then, and things could get messy." Before Ella could say another world, the scary Godmother vanished in a cloud of green smoke.

Ella blasted to the ball, landing on the palace balcony. This really impressed the Prince and he immediately asked her to dance. They danced one dance after another and by midnight were madly in love. Ella knew it was midnight because when the Prince brought her a cup of punch her nose dropped into it with a loud *plop*!

"Oh, no! I have to go!" she cried. Covering the

hole in her face with one hand. Ella turned and raced to get her jetpack.

"Wait!" cried the Prince hurrying to stop her. As Ella blasted off in the air, the prince caught hold of her left foot. To his shock, it came off in his hand! He called out, "Come back. You forgot something!"

For days, the prince went from house to house clutching the severed foot, trying to find his mysterious maiden. Finally his journey took him to Ella's door but no one answered his knock. Just as he turned to go, he saw a girl in rags hopping about the side garden chasing a squirrel. The girl had only one foot.

"My love!" he cried, waving her missing body part in the air. "I have brought you your foot. Put it on and marry me!"

"But Prince, I can't marry you," Ella said. "I'm a zombie! A monster!"

The prince smiled, revealing a shining pair of fangs. "Darling, I'm a vampire." He shrugged. "Nobody's perfect."

And so the Prince and Zombie-rella were married and were monstrously happy forever after. Even Ella's wicked stepsisters were happy. They got their own reality show—"Desperate Step-sisters"—that is still running to this day.

THE END

FEAR FACTor: *Scholionophobia* is an extreme fear of school based on past experience.

BLOODY BAND-AIDS

Here's a tasty treat for those times when you want to truly horrify friends or family members.

WHAT YOU NEED:

- Plate
- Small spoon
- Butter knife
- 2 whole graham crackers
- 2 tablespoons cream cheese
- 1 tablespoon seedless red jelly (strawberry works well)

WHAT TO DO:

1. Break each graham cracker into four rectangles, using the lines cut into them as a guide. (If they don't break evenly, eat them and try again.)

2. Spread a square of cream cheese into the center of each cracker. (That will be the absorbent white cushion part of the Band-Aid.)

3. Drop a small splotch of red jelly (blood) into the middle of each cream-cheese cushion.

4. Serve your treats on a plate garnished with a real box of Band-Aids so your friends know exactly what they're enjoying.

BODY BREAKDOWN

· ·

Warning: the following step-by-step look at how the body decomposes may require a strong stomach.

- Just after death, the body stiffens, first at the jaws and neck. After 48 hours, the corpse relaxes and muscles sag.

- Blood settles in the part of the body closest to the ground, turning the rest of the body pale.

- After two to three days, the skin turns green. The body's enzymes start to eat through cell walls, and the liquid inside leaks out.

- Bacteria feed on the liquid and release sulfur gas. With nowhere to go, the gas causes the corpse to bloat and swell (and sometimes burst).

- By the end of the third day, the skin changes from green to purple to black. This stage is called *autolysis*, which means "self-digestion."

- Next comes "skin slip." As cells continue to break down, liquid continues to leak. After about a week, the skin loosens and starts to peel off in large chunks.

- After two weeks, the fluid leaks from the nose and mouth. After three weeks, teeth and nails loosen; internal organs start to rupture.

- After about a month, the corpse dissolves and sinks into the ground, leaving only the skeletal remains.

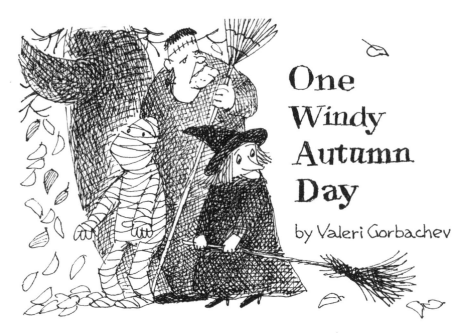

One Windy Autumn Day

by Valeri Gorbachev

One windy autumn day, Frankenstein was cleaning up his backyard.

CREEPY COMIC HEROES

· · · · · · · · · · · · · · · · · · · ·

In our book, the odder the comic character, the better!

MADAME FATAL

FIRST APPEARED: Crack Comics #1 (1940)

PROFILE: Madame Fatal has gray hair, wears a red hood, and walks with a cane. But she can kick some serious butt! That's because this "old lady" is really a middle-aged man named Richard Stanton in disguise. He is a wealthy world-famous actor who infiltrates gangs by disguising himself as Madame Fatal. (Who wouldn't trust a nice old lady?) Then Madame Fatal surprises the bad guys with her superior strength (and the cane)!

ARM-FALL-OFF-BOY

FIRST APPEARED: DC Comics, Vol. 2 #46, (1989)

PROFILE: File this superhero in the "What were they thinking?" department. Arm-Fall-Off-Boy's name says it all: He can remove his limbs and then put them back on again. That's it. (Whenever he removes an arm or a leg, it makes a "plorp" sound.)

DR. LEMONET

FIRST APPEARED: The Vault of Horror #13 (1950)

PROFILE: This dark tale, called "Doctor of Horror," takes place in the 17th century. Dr. LeMonet is an anatomy teacher at a respected college. But he's run into a problem: There aren't enough dead bodies available for his medical students to experiment on. And if the good doctor can't find more bodies, he'll lose his job. That's why he becomes a grave robber. But when the graveyard runs out of freshly-dead bodies, Dr. LeMonet decides it's time to make some new freshly-dead bodies.

BIG BERTHA

FIRST APPEARED: Marvel Comics "West Coast Avengers" #46 (1985)

PROFILE: Ashley Crawford is a mutant shapeshifter from Wisconsin who made her fortune by taking the form of a 120-pound, beautiful supermodel. But when trouble arises, she becomes Big Bertha, a 750-pound woman who fights for good. Big Bertha's giant belly can deflect bullets and buses. She can even jump from a high building and bounce her way to safety. The superhero Deadpool has a crush on Big Bertha…but not on Ashley Crawford. When Big Bertha lectures Deadpool about judging people only by their looks, he takes his off his mask to reveal his disgusting, diseased face. Then, ignoring her own advice, Big Bertha barfs.

• • •

Q: How does the Wolfman walk through walls?
A: He uses the door.

Q: What sign does a vacationing plumber leave on his door?
A: Gone flushing.

THE BLACK DOG

. . . .

An Uncle John's Eerily Twisted Tale.

ALL MACAULEY CREEVERS had ever wanted
was a dog. Even before he could talk, his favorite
toy was a stuffed puppy with matted fur. By the time he
turned six, he began to realize that his dreams of playing
fetch in the front yard or going on long hikes on the trails
behind his home might never come true. His parents, you
see, were not what you might call "animal people."

They had done a good job of hiding it from
Macauley for the first few years of his life. But when
he asked when they were getting a dog, he noticed his
parents would become uneasy and exchange glances that
seemed to mean more than the "we'll see" answer they
gave. As he got older, he noticed how his mother would
stiffen when even the friendliest dog approached. She
would sometimes give the dog a polite pat on the head.
But he'd never seen her crouch down and give any dog a
nice long "Who is a good boy?" sort of scratch.

And his dad? Well, Macauley realized that he
would never have a dog to call his own on the day that
his father discovered that the Hansons' dog had been
drinking out of the decorative fountain in their yard
again. The dog had licked it dry and the pump had
sputtered air for so long that its motor burned out.

"I HATE DOGS!" Mr. Creevers howled. "I've had it up to HERE with people letting their dogs traipse around our yard like they own the place!"

"Me, too!" his mom had shrieked. "Dogs smell like old socks and they have fleas and ticks and-and communicable diseases!" Mrs. Creevers shuddered.

As Macauley listened to his parents yell and scream about the various reasons why dogs were so terrible, he let his lifelong dream of having one to call his own fade away. Then his mom turned around and saw him standing there. Her lips trembled. "I'm sorry, son," she said. Your father and I just aren't animal people."

The next day, Macauley's parents showed up with a car full of camping equipment, which was pretty weird since they weren't camping people, either.

"What's going on, Dad?" he asked.

"We're going camping!" His dad gave him a big fake grin. "You've always wanting to go camping, right?"

"Uh, sure." MacCauley nodded.

"Then hop aboard." His dad waved.

A few hours later, rain started pelting the windshield. "I sure hope that the weatherman was right about this storm passing through dear." Mrs. Creever frowned at the pounding rain. After a long and twisty drive, the Creevers finally arrived at their campsite. "We're going to have to move fast to get this camp set up before nightfall, gang!" Mr. Creevers was already unpacking the tent and poles. Macauley started to open a box with an air mattress inside, but his mom grabbed it. "I'll take care of that," she said. "Now that the rain's stopped, you should go, uh," she glanced over her shoulder with wide eyes, "enjoy n-nature or something."

MacCauley grabbed a flashlight and headed toward the trailhead across from their campsite. The woods seemed strangely silent after the rain, except for water dripping from the branches. He heard what might have been someone shouting, or maybe an owl hooting in the distance. As he rounded a curve in the trail, Mac froze. There, just a few feet away, stood a dog so black it almost blended with the shadows beneath the trees.

"Hey, boy!" Mac held out a hand. "You lost?" He figured the dog had wandered away from one of the campsites. "Don't worry, boy," Mac said. "We'll find your owners. Come here!"

But instead of coming toward him, the dog turned away. Within seconds, it had disappeared into the forest. "Hey!" Mac called. "Come back here!" He flipped on his flashlight and pointed the beam under the trees. At that moment, the dog looked back over its shoulder. Its eyes glowed bright as fresh blood. Mac started to back up, slowly—step by step. "It's okay, B-Buddy," he stuttered. "You go wherever you want to." But at that moment, the black dog with the glowing red eyes whined, just like any dog separated from its owner might whine, and Mac's heart melted.

"Okay," he said. "Let's go." Mac followed the black dog deeper and deeper into the woods. Soon, he heard rushing water and felt a wet chill creeping over him.

Up ahead, he spotted a ghostly mist coming from what might have been a creek. As he got closer, he saw that the wooden bridge that crossed the creek had collapsed. A girl hung there, clinging to a board while raging white water tried to pull her into the torrent.

"Hey!" Mac hurried forward. "Hey, you okay?"

"Help me!" the girl yelped. "I-I don't think I can hold on much longer."

Mac looked around frantically for something that would help. Then he heard scratching. He spotted the black dog's eyes glowing red beneath the underbrush. It was pawing at a thick branch. "Good boy!" Mac grinned. He grabbed the branch, sat down behind a rock at the edge of the creek, and planted his feet on it. Then he reached the branch toward the girl. A few minutes and a lot of tugging later, she was gasping on the bank. When she caught her breath, she looked at Mac with grateful eyes. "Thank you *so* much," she said. "If you hadn't showed up, I'd be dead now."

Mac shook his head. "Don't thank me. Thank your dog. He led me here."

The girl's eyes went wide. "My dog? No. No he couldn't have."

"But he did." Mac assured her.

"What did he look like?"

"Big," said Mac. "And black as night."

The girl's lips trembled. "Nightmare. That's his name."

"Cool," said Mac.

"He was a good dog."

She's in shock, Mac decided. "*Is*, right? You mean he *is* a good dog." But then the girl sat up, turned back toward the creek, and pointed. In the middle of the creek, Mac saw a body caught between two boulders: the body of a large black Lab. The rushing water rocked it gently, but it was clear that the big black dog was dead.

After a long quiet minute, the girl sniffed. "You're right," she said. "He *is* a good dog. Even after death."

Two days later, MacCauley's parents took him to the shelter to pick out a dog. He found a big black one with sad lonely eyes. "I'm going to call him Wisht," he told his parents.

"Wisht?" His parents looked puzzled.

"Because he's just what I've always wished for," said MacCauley.

MacCauley's mother reached out to pat the dog's head. "If he keeps you safe like Nightmare did his owner, he's just what we wish for, too." The she stuck her hand in her purse and rumbled around for her hand sanitizer.

"Don't worry, Wisht." Mac ruffled the dog's fur. "My parents are weird, but they mean well."

THE END

"There will one day spring from the brain of science a machine or force so fearful in its potentialities, so absolutely terrifying, that even man, the fighter, who will dare torture and death in order to inflict torture and death, will be appalled, and so abandon war forever."

—**Thomas A. Edison**

TOP 10 PHOBIAS

· ·

*Sweaty palms…racing heartbeat…an overwhelming
feeling of dread…. Which of these Top 10 fears
would send YOU over the edge?*

1. BATS! Afraid of creatures with dark, leathery wings?
Then you have *chiroptophobia*—fear of bats. *Never
fear!* Even though you've probably seen Dracula turn
into a bat in scary movies, in real life that just doesn't
happen. Even the dreaded vampire bat mostly feeds
on cattle and horse blood—rarely on humans. Most
bats are beneficial animals, pollinating the rainforest,
distributing the seeds of fruits such as bananas and
mangos in their poop, and eating insects—lots of
insects. A colony of 30 million bats in Texas eats 250
tons of insects every night. (Maybe bugs are the ones
who should have chiroptophobia!)

2. VAMPIRES! *Sanguivoriphobia*—the fear of "blood
eaters"—has been around since the Middle Ages
(A.D. 1066–1485). Back then, misfortunes like a
drought or a crop failure or a dread disease were
blamed on vampires. *Never fear!* Vampires don't exist.
(Really. They don't.) So why did people believe in
them? A lack of knowledge about what happens to
a body when it decays helped fuel vampire stories

in medieval times. Villagers would dig up recently buried bodies as they searched for the vampire causing all the trouble. Sometimes they found grisly "evidence." For example, a body might have had intestinal decomposition—meaning its guts were rotting. That can cause blood to travel to the mouth of the corpse, which was seen as "proof" that the vampire had been found.

3. STORMS! If storms have you diving under the bed you probably have *astraphobia*, fear of lightning and *brontophobia*, fear of thunder. Lightning can be dangerous: on average, 52 people are killed and over 300 injured every year by lightning strikes. But there are ways to stay safe. If you can't count to 30 between the lightning flash and the thunder boom, then the lightning is close enough to be a danger. Move away from water—even puddles. Don't stand under tall trees, especially a lone tree in the middle of a field. Stay away from wide-open spaces where you're the tallest object. Don't climb a mountain, or, if you're already on a mountain, try to get below the tree line. And avoid touching metal until the storm ends.

4. REPTILES! *Herpetophobia* is a fear of reptiles. It comes from the Greek word *herpeton* which means "creeping creature." Most of the 6500 species of reptiles pose no threat to people but some of them are worth a few goosebumps. The Nile crocodile is believed to kill around 200 people a year. Venomous snakes kill approximately 20,000 people a year worldwide: 14,000 in Southeast Asia alone. And in Indonesia two Komodo dragons waitied patiently under a tree to maul a fruit picker to death (Now *that's* scary!).

5. BURIED ALIVE! George Washington is best known as the first president of the United States. But he also suffered from *taphephobia*—a fear of being buried alive. If this is your fear, you don't have as much to worry about as George. Before modern embalming methods, people were buried quickly after being pronounced dead. Unfortunately some of them weren't actually dead. In 1852, George Bateson patented the "Bateson's Belfry." It was a coffin with a bell inside that could be rung by pulling a cord—just in case… *(Read more about this fear on page 213.)*

6. GRAVES! Does the idea of visiting a graveyard give you chills? Then you may have *coimetrophobia*, the fear of cemeteries. A similar phobia is *placophobia*— the fear of gravestones. (Especially one with your name on it!)

7. THE DARK! If you have *nyctophobia*, you're not alone. A recent study showed that even adults are afraid of the dark: at least, about half of them are. Fear of the dark may go back to the beginnings of human history. Many predators hunt at night—and some of them hunted our human ancestors. So fear of the dark was a survival strategy. Today? Statistics show that between 60 and 70 percent of crimes happen after dark. So it's no surprise that, for some, the fear of being hunted at night remains strong.

8. VEGGIES? Not all phobias are about graveyards and bats and slithery things. There are plenty of other things to be horrified about. "I have always had an irrational fear of vegetables," says Vicki Larrieux of Great Britain. "Even as a child I used to properly freak out if some carrots or a few peas were on my plate." If you're like Vicki then you have *lachanophobia.*

9. PUBLIC POTTIES! Can you only "go" at home? Then maybe you have *paruresis,* the fear of public restrooms. *Never fear!* "One of the cleanest things in bathrooms are the toilet seats," says Charles Gerba, a microbiologist at the University of Arizona says. "I'd put my fanny on it anytime—unless it's wet; then you'd want to wipe it first."

10. BEDTIME! Not wanting to go to bed is one thing, but being afraid to go to bed? That's a whole different bedtime story. There's a name for it: *clinophobia.* And it's the irrational fear of going to bed or falling to sleep. Why fear bedtime? Some people have *sleep apnea,* a medical condition that slows or even stops a person's breathing during sleep. (Scary!) Some fear dying in their sleep. Others fear nightmares. If that's your big bedtime fear, then Uncle John wishes you... sweet dreams!

PURPLE PEE-PLE

. . . .

On page 97, we told you about a blood disease that can give humans that "wolfman" look. Here's a form of the disease with royal roots.

- Porphyria is a group of diseases caused by a buildup of porphyrins (red and purple pigments) in the body.
- Europe's royal houses of Stuart, Hanover, and Prussia have passed the faulty gene that causes porphyria from generation to generation.
- Pee the color of port wine is one symptom of too many red and purple pigments in the body.
- King James I of England probably had porphyria. His doctor wrote a note describing the king's urine as being "purple as Alicante Wine."
- England's "Mad King" George III wasn't insane after all. He had the classic "purple pee" symptom of porphyria. The disease interrupts nerve impulses to the brain and can cause everything from confusion to delusions. At one point, George held conversations with angels (or so the deluded king thought).
- Queen Victoria's granddaughter Charlotte wrote in her letters of having dark red urine. By scraping a bit of bone marrow from her skeleton, researchers proved that she had porphyria, "beyond a shadow of a doubt."
- One out of every two royals who have the faulty gene will pass it down to their children.

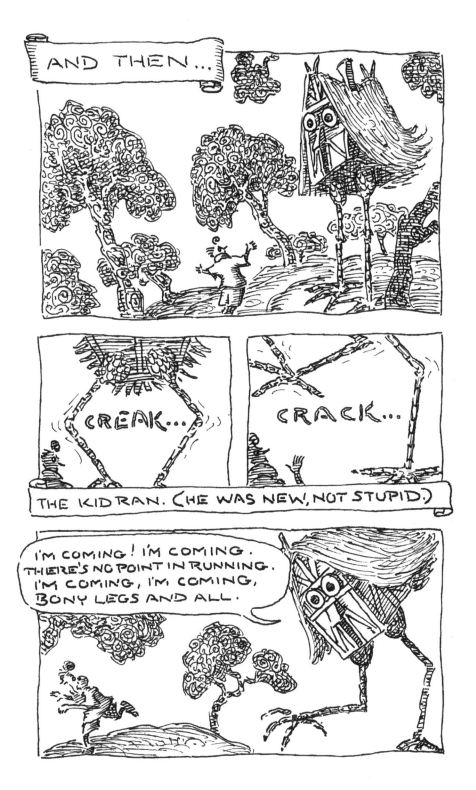

DEADLY WEATHER

. . . .

Zombie apocalypse? Not gonna happen.
Monster storms that make sci-fi scares look like
a sunny day in the park? Oh, yeah!

SUPER TYPHOON NINA

1975's Super Typhoon Nina dumped 42 inches of
rain—a year's worth—on central China in 24 hours.
The deluge collapsed two dams designed to protect the
region…against heavy rainfall. The Banqiao Dam could
resist a 1,000-year flood—11.8 inches in one day. The
Shimantan Dam could hold enough water to fill 28,000
Olympic swimming pools. But Nina dumped 7.5 inches
of rainfall *per hour* into the reservoirs. When the dams
failed, a wall of water 20 feet high and 7.5 miles wide
surged down the river channel at speeds near 31 mph.
The floods swept away 86,000 people and submerged
thousands of square miles of land. Nina collapsed 6
million buildings, affected 11 million people, and cause
$1.2 billion in damage. That puts Nina at the top of the
list of destructive typhoons.

BLIZZARD OF 1993

At its height, the blizzard of '93, or Superstorm '93,
stretched from Canada into Central America, but
its main impact was on the Eastern United States.

The storm raged for three days, from March 12 to 14. It paralyzed the eastern seaboard with record cold temperatures, snowfall, and winds.

Tennessee received the most snow—a whopping 56 inches. Along the shores of Long Island, New York, pounding waves tumbled 18 houses into the sea. In Florida, the storm spawned 15 tornadoes and killed 44 people. The Gulf of Mexico and Atlantic Ocean churned, and the Coast Guard rescued 160 people. But 48 more were still missing at sea when the storm ended. Overall, the storm's surge, snows, winds, and tornadoes damaged or destroyed 18,000 homes and killed 285 people. It's been called "The Storm of the Century."

HURRICANE KATRINA

Hurricane Katrina made landfall near New Orleans, Louisiana, on August 29, 2005. The monster storm hovered over the region for seven terrifying hours. Winds of up to 145 mph ripped buildings to shreds. A 20-foot storm surge sent water pounding through canals and surging over levees. Then…the battered levees crumbled. "There was water on the street, then the sidewalk, then water in the house," one survivor told *The Times-Picayune*.

Water rose fast in low-lying neighborhoods near levees, such as the Lower Ninth Ward. Daniel Weber tried to pull his wife onto the roof of their house. "My hands were all cut up from breaking through the window to escape," he said. Weber and his wife both went under. She never surfaced. He grabbed a piece of driftwood and hung on for 14 hours before being rescued.

When the hurricane ended, 80 percent of New Orleans was under water. Though New Orleans had been nearly wiped off the map, Hurricane Katrina also affected 90,000 square miles of land in Louisiana, Mississippi, and Alabama. At least 1,800 people died during the nightmare storm. Bodies continued to be found in condemned homes eight months later. More than 700 people are still reported missing.

• • •

REDNECK RODENT ROAST

How many rednecks does it take to turn an apartment complex into a smoking ruin? Just one, as long as he has a propane torch on hand. According to Fire Chief Jim Kohsel, a resident on the third floor of the Clear View Apartments in Holland Township, Michigan, wanted to cook up a squirrel for dinner. But first, he decided to burn off the rodent's fur...with a propane torch. Not a good idea. The squirrel's fur burned just fine, but so did the wooden deck beneath the animal and the surrounding apartments. By the time the fire department put out the flames, 32 apartments had smoke damage and 8 had been totally toasted.

"The piano is a monster that screams when you touch its teeth."

—Andrés Segovia

TERROR
IN THE WATER

· ·

Whether you swim in oceans, lakes, or rivers, seriously
scary creatures might be sharing the water with you.

VIPERFISH

The first thing you notice about this fierce predator
is its fangs—they are so long, they curve out of its mouth
and all the way back to its eyeballs. The spine of this
two-foot-long fish is tipped with a *photophore*, an organ
that actually lights up. The viperfish floats motionless in
the totally dark depths of the ocean, waving a long lure
in front of its mouth that blinks on and off like a neon
sign. Unsuspecting shrimp, anchovies, mackerel, and
other fish are attracted by the light and swim toward it.
In a flash, the viperfish sinks its fangs into dinner. If the
prey is too big for its mouth, no problem—the viperfish's
skull has a hinge that allows it to open its mouth wider
and…wider…and wider…to swallow bigger fish.

SNAKEHEAD FISH

This monster fish has a huge mouth with short spiky teeth
and a monster appetite to match. A single snakehead fish
can eat every living thing in a pond or lake, including
plankton, carp, snails, and frogs. What's really bizarre is
when the food runs out, the snakehead fish climbs out

of the pond and crawls off in search of another pond, eating frogs, mice, rats, and small birds on its way. This prehistoric-looking fish can grow to be 3 feet long and weigh as much as 15 pounds. But no matter how attractive that may sound, you can't have one for a pet. Because they can wipe out entire populations of fish, snakeheads are illegal to own.

VANDELLIA FISH

This little sucker lives in freshwater streams like the Amazon River in South America. The vandellia fish is so teeny—2.5 centimeters long by 3.5 centimeters wide—it's practically invisible. Yet it is one of the most feared fish in the world. Why? It is attracted to urine. Unlucky people who happen to pee in the Amazon River discover (the hard way) that this tiny fish can follow the stream of urine back into their body. What's even worse, once the vandellia fish gets inside its victim, it extends the short sharp spines that cover its gills and locks itself in place. Then it hungrily sucks the person's blood and gnaws holes in its victim's blood vessels. If not removed (by surgery), this spiny bloodsucker can cause shock and death. (Note to self: Never pee in the Amazon River!)

●   ●   ●

"For millions of years, mankind lived just like the animals. Then something happened which unleashed the power of our imagination. We learned to talk and we learned to listen."—**Stephen Hawking, cosmologist**

WE ALL FALL DOWN

. . . .

Introducing: The gory beginnings of favorite kids' games.

RING AROUND THE ROSIE

In the 1300s, a disease called the bubonic plague killed nearly a third of the population of Europe— around 25 million people. Also known as the black death, the plague was spread by fleas, rats, and sneezing people. It was almost always fatal. You may not realize it, but you've probably been singing about the plague since kindergarten. The fateful words?

Ring around the rosie,
A pocket full of posies,
Ashes, ashes,
We all fall down.

"Ring around the rosie" was a reference to the red rash that was the first symptom of the plague. The round red "buboes" were inflamed glands that were filled with infectious fluid.

"Posies" are flowers. In the Middle Ages, many people thought pleasant smells could fight off disease. So they carried flowers, which also might have masked the smell of dead bodies. Other versions of the song refer to "pots full" of posies, or even "bottles full."

"Ashes" probably was the sound for a sneeze, like the

ah-choo we say today. (Some versions even say *ah-choo* instead.) Chills, fever, and upset stomachs were other signs of the plague.

"We all fall down"? Well, that was a nod to the many people who were dying. Gruesome, but clever, no?

LONDON BRIDGE

In "London Bridge," the falling down refers to the collapse of a bridge. In 1014, London Bridge was the city's only bridge over the River Thames. King Olaf of Norway—an ally of the English King—used his longships to pull down the bridge and send an invading Danish army into the river. Other bridges over the river have burned down or collapsed since then, and the song might be based on one of those. There are more than 20 verses of the song, and several versions of the game that goes with it. The first verse goes like this:

London Bridge is falling down,
Falling down, falling down.
London Bridge is falling down,
My fair lady.

No one is sure who the "fair lady" is, but one rumor is that a woman was once buried alive in the bridge.

•　　•　　•

FEAR FACTOR: In 2010, there were 15 U.S. citizens killed in terrorist attacks. Killed by falling televisions that same year: 16.

STINKPOT

· · · · · · · · · · · · · · · · · · · ·

An Uncle John's Eerily Twisted Tale!

OLD MRS. RATWICH loved her kitty, Stinkpot. She was the only person in the world who did. Stinkpot had mangy patchy hair. His whiskers were crooked, his ears torn, and he had lost an eye to a fight with a raccoon. But for an elderly lady living on Social Security checks, Stinkpot was the perfect pet. Why? Because he wasn't a finicky eater like most cats. No. Stinkpot gobbled up anything she put on his china dish: slugs, mouse carcasses, rotten tomatoes, milk so sour it was thick and yellow. He gobbled up decaying halibut heads she found in the fish market dumpster and whiffy chicken wings she found in the trash behind the local bar.

"Nothing's too good for my kitty," Mrs. Ratwich would always say as she gave Stinkpot a pat. Her reward? A rumbling purr that reeked of all the horrible things Stinkpot had gobbled up.

One day—we're sorry to say—Stinkpot choked to death on a chicken bone. "Poor kitty," murmured Mrs. Ratwich as she carried his body down to the dirt-floored cellar and buried him. Then she went back upstairs to her lonely house.

Early the next morning—"Meowr!"

Mrs. Ratwich sat straight up in bed. "Stinkpot?"

she called. "Is that you?"

"Meeowrrr!" The second call was louder—more insistent. Mrs. Ratwich threw on her robe and hurried to the cellar door. She opened it a crack, flipped up the light switch, and peered down the steps. The cellar was cold and dark and quiet. "I must be imagining things," Mrs. Ratwich told herself. "But I'll set out a little dish of food. Just in case." She searched the kitchen trash and found a blackened banana that she placed on a china saucer. "Here, kitty!" Mrs. Ratwich called. Then she set the saucer on the top step and closed the cellar door.

The next morning, she heard it again: "Meeeowrrr!" When Mrs. Ratwich opened the cellar door, she saw the banana was gone. She ventured down the stairs to check—had Stinkpot been buried alive and dug himself out? No. Stinkpot's grave was just as she'd left it. "I may just be a silly old lady," she muttered as she set a loaf of mildewed bread on the china dish, "but he sounds so hungry."

Every morning, Mrs. Ratwich would hear louder and louder cries from the cellar, and she would set out larger and larger treats on the step. She set out mushy apples, slimy chicken bones, and cheese gone green with mold. She set out old salami, putrid pastrami, and a squirrel squashed flat by a bus. But no matter how much "food" she put on the top step, the next morning it would be gone and the next day's "Meowrrr!" would be louder and sound hungrier.

Mrs. Ratwich did not know what to do, so she decided to make herself a cup of tea. Tea always helped her think. As she ran the water to fill the kettle, she noticed that the drain was clogged up. "I guess I'll have to call a plumber."

The plumber showed up in stained overalls and picked at his teeth with dirty fingernails. He eyed Mrs. Ratwich's kitchen sink. "This is going to be expensive."

"But it's just a clog," Mrs. Ratwich said. "How expensive can it be?"

"Five hundred bucks," said the plumber.

"That's ridiculous," said Mrs. Ratwich.

"Look, you old bag of bones, clogs like this cause problems you don't even want to think about. This ain't no time to be cheap."

Mrs. Ratwich was about to tell the obnoxious plumber to get out of her kitchen when she heard a familiar "Meowrrr" coming from the cellar. She put on her best grandmotherly smile. "You're the expert."

The plumber had the sink unclogged in three minutes flat. "Where's my money?" he demanded.

"It's downstairs—buried the cellar," said Mrs. Ratwich. "I don't believe in banks. But you'll have to dig it up yourself. This old bag of bones is too worn out."

The plumber sneered. "I'll get it."

"I'm sure you will," said Mrs. Ratwich, closing the cellar door quickly after him.

Mrs. Ratwich made her tea. As she took her first sip, she heard an enormous happy purr rumble from the cellar. "You're welcome, Stinkpot," she said.

THE END

TAKE A BITE OUT OF TRANSYLVANIA

∙∙∙∙∙∙∙∙∙∙∙∙∙∙∙∙∙∙∙∙∙∙

"Transylvania is not England. Our ways are not your ways, and there shall be to you many strange things."
—from Bram Stoker's classic vampire tale, Dracula

FANGS FOR THE HOSPITALITY

When the fictional Count Dracula welcomed Jonathan Harker to his Transylvania castle, the young lawyer from London thought he was there to settle a property deal. Sure, he wondered why that woman at the Golden Krone Hotel had begged him not to travel on the eve of St. George's Day and had made him take along a crucifix and cloves of garlic. Of course he found it odd that his host with the pointy teeth never shared a meal with him and was never around during the day—who wouldn't? But he had no idea what horrors lay in store for him.

GRUESOME TWOSOME

Was Dracula for real or did Bram Stoker make him up? The author based his character on a real Romanian prince named Vlad Dracula (1431–1476). Vlad was the warlord of the Romanian province of Wallachia. His dad, Vlad Basareb, adopted the name, "Dracul," when he was inducted into the Order of the Dracul, or "Dragon." So young Vlad went by the name "Dracula"—which means "son of Dracul."

Unlike the fictional Dracula, Vlad Dracula didn't go around the country sucking people's blood. However, he had an equally chilling way to frighten away enemies—he impaled them on stakes. In 1462, one Turkish sultan ordered his soldiers to retreat after they stumbled upon a "forest" of impaled bodies outside the gates of Wallachia's capital.

Vlad's method of torture and slow death earned him the name, "Vlad Tepes," or "Vlad the Impaler." Romanians consider him a national hero, because he defended Wallachia—a Romanian province—against the Ottoman Empire. Which Dracula was creepier, the vampire or the impaler? Time for some on-site research.

STAKING OUT DRACULA

After visiting all the Count Dracula sites in England, travel writer Steven P. Unger headed to Transylvania, the historical region in the central part of Romania, to continue his "obsession" with all things Dracula. His goal: visit every site related to the fictional Count Dracula or his historical counterpart, Vlad Tepes. Like the fictional Jonathan Harker, Unger kept a travel journal that ended up in a book. Unlike Harker, Unger didn't have to travel alone. The Romanian Tourist Board encourages Dracula fans to visit both the fictional settings of the novel and the real sites made famous by the Impaler. Since the 1980s, visitors can even sign up for Dracula-themed tours. So Unger had plenty of company as he visited these sites:

- **Bistrita (or Bistritz)** This town at the foot of the Borgo Pass in northern Romania was the fictional Jonathan Harker's last stop before he took his fateful journey to meet the count. On May 3, Harker spent the night at the Hotel Golden Krone (compliments of his yet-unseen host). No such hotel existed in Bram Stoker's day. But, in the 1980s, the town built one. To duplicate Harker's evening meal, the hotel restaurant serves something called a "robber steak."

- **Borgo Pass (or Tihuta Pass)** To reach the count's castle, Harker took a horse-drawn passenger coach to the top of the Borgo Pass. "As we wound on our endless way, and the sun sank lower and lower behind us," he recalled, "the shadows of the evening began to creep round us." After the coach reached the crest, another coach driven by a man with "bright eyes" conveyed Harper to his destination.

- **Hotel Castel Dracula** Built in the 1980s, this vampire-themed hotel stands at the setting of the fictional Count Dracula's castle. Some visitors find the blood-red carpets, stuffed wolves in the lobby, and fake crypt with a coffin kind of tacky. But it has great views of the Carpathian mountains.

- **Vlad Dracul's House (Casa Dracula), Sighisoara** In 1431, Prince Vlad was born in this house at Strada

Cositorarilor Number 5. He lived here until he was four. A wrought-iron dragon hangs at the entrance. A medieval weapons museum fills most of the first floor.

- **Targoviste** When Vlad's dad became ruler of Wallachia, Vlad's family moved to this provincial capital. Following in his father's footsteps, young Vlad returned there as warlord from 1456 to 1462.

- **Poienari (the "real" Castle of Dracula)** Scholars believe that Bram Stoker used Poienari—Prince Vlad's fortress overlooking Targoviste—as his model for Count Dracula's castle. The climb to the top of the ruins is a long one: 1462 steps. From his perch there, Vlad once watched the mass impaling of 20,000 Turkish prisoners.

DRACULA HUNTER'S LANGUAGE LESSON

Before you start chasing the Count, arm yourself with a few words and phrases you can count on.

English	Romanian
Do you speak English?	*Vorbesti engleza?*
Do you have the time?	*Aveti timp?*
I'm lost!	*M'am ratacit!*
No	*Nu*
Blood transfusion	*Transfuzie de sange*
Neck	*Gat*
Teeth	*Dinti*
And the most important word...	
Help!	*Ajutor!*

TICK-TOCK,
MUMMY'S IN THE CLOCK

. . . .

On page 213 we told you how freaked out Victorians were about being buried alive. This lady had no intention of waking up in some nasty crypt or coffin.

UPON HER DEATH in 1758, a wealthy spinster named Hannah Beswick left 20,000 guineas to her doctor (about 10 million dollars today). There was one condition: she must *never* be buried. Dr. Charles White did his best. He embalmed his deceased patient and kept her body amongst his anatomical specimens. Every day for several years, he checked Miss Beswick for signs of life, as detailed in her will. Later, he placed her mummified remains in a grandfather clock, opening it once a year to check on his oldest patient—until he himself passed away.

When Dr. White died, Miss Beswick's mummy was moved to the Manchester Natural History Museum, where it was placed on public display until 1867. At that time, Hannah Beswick was declared "irrevocably and unmistakably dead," and her body was laid to rest.

Beswick's wasn't the only death-insuring request:
- British rare book dealer Francis Douce left 200 guineas to a surgeon to remove his heart upon his death.
- Author Harriet Martineau left her personal physician 10 pounds to cut off her head.

THE BOUNCING EYEBALL

· ·

One day in his mad-science lab, Dr. Johnenstein dropped his lunch (a hard-boiled egg) into a beaker filled with vinegar and forgot all about it. Here's how to replicate his results.

WHAT YOU NEED:

- Hard-boiled egg (in shell)
- White vinegar
- Clear jar or glass
- Waterproof black marker

WHAT TO DO:

1. Place a hard-boiled egg into the jar or glass. Pour enough white vinegar into the container to cover the egg completely. Let the covered egg sit for two full days in a dark place where it won't be disturbed.

2. Remove the egg from the container. Rinse it gently under cold running water until it's clean. Carefully pat it dry and draw a pupil and iris on it with the black waterproof marker. Let the eyeball sit at room temperature for a few hours until it's completely dry.

3. Now comes the fun part. Hold the eyeball about a foot above the top of a table or counter, then drop it. Play around with dropping the eyeball from different heights to find out how to get the best bounce.

DR. JOHNENSTEIN SAYS: When you immerse an egg in vinegar, the acid in the vinegar reacts with the calcium in the egg's shell and begins to eat it away. After a few days, the reaction is complete, and the egg is left with a waxy membrane and no shell. *Boing!*

•　•　•

A HAUNTED OUTHOUSE

And now, the outhouse story you've all been waiting for!

WE SEARCHED FAR AND WIDE for an eyewitness account of a haunted outhouse. (If you know about one, send us your story!) We did find this: A legend about Oakey Streak Methodist Episcopal Church in Red Level, Alabama. The church has been abandoned for many years. Many locals say the grounds are haunted—including the raggedy outhouse out back. If you go inside, the ghost locks you in from the outside. You can yell, scream, and bang on the door, but it won't let you out. The only way to escape is for a living person to open the door from the outside. So if you want to investigate the old outhouse at the abandoned church, don't go alone!

For more tales of ghosts in our favorite room, see page 47.

DEATH-DEFYING
DAREDEVIL

· · · · · · · · · · · · · · · · · · · ·

Is this guy mind-blowingly brave or just nuts?

SPEED DEMONS

In 1947, Air Force pilot Charles "Chuck" Yeager shook the world when he broke the sound barrier in his rocket-powered airplane. Yeager bulleted across the Mojave Desert at 807 miles per hour. On October 14, 2012, Austrian daredevil Felix Baumgartner trumped Yeager big time—65 years to the day—by hurling *himself* through the sound barrier from a spot 24 miles above planet Earth. He plummeted Earthward at supersonic speeds of up to 833 mph, with nothing but a 100-pound pressurized spacesuit to protect him. (Nuts, right?)

Like Yeager's flight, Baumgartner's jump happened above the desert. The spot? Roswell, New Mexico, made famous by U.F.O. sightings in 1947. Baumgartner was strapped inside a closet-sized space capsule and lifted by an enormous helium balloon toward the jump point. The capsule climbed for two hours. And then Felix opened the capsule's steel door. Breathing heavily, he eyed the speckled ball of Earth where 8 million people sat watching the jump live on YouTube. In a staticky voice, Baumgartner said, "I wish the whole world could see what I see."

CALL ME BOND

Most of us would never consider jumping from a capsule even one mile above Earth, much less 24 miles. But for Felix Baumgartner death-defying leaps are the norm. He started dreaming of sky-diving when he was little, and made his first jump at age 16. Before that helium balloon pulled him into near-Earth orbit, he'd already landed more than 2,500 ridiculously high leaps from statues, bridges, and the world's tallest skyscrapers.

In 1999, Baumgartner wanted to set a record by leaping off what was then the world's tallest building—the Petronas Towers in Kuala Lumpur. Here's the catch: It's not legal to hurl yourself from buildings. So Baumgartner pulled a few James Bond-type moves: He carried a fake I.D. and a briefcase to disguise himself as a businessman. Then he walked right past the tower's security guards, rode the elevator to the 88th floor, took his parachute and camcorder from the briefcase, climbed to the end of a window-washing crane, and jumped. The nearly 1,500-foot leap set a world record for highest building jump. And Baumgartner captured the whole thing on video on his way down.

STOP THE BALLOON! I WANT TO GET OFF

Baumgartner's leap through the sound barrier nearly got grounded. The problem? Felix was used to feeling the wind during jumps, but the pressurized suit and helmet designed by NASA felt like a full-body cast. He couldn't feel the wind, so he didn't know how to move his body against it. Result: panic attacks. It took a sports psychologist to help Baumgartner get the mind control he needed to go through with the jump.

Psyching himself up wasn't all the daredevil had to rely on for the jump: he also had the voice of 82-year-old retired Air Force colonel Joe Kittinger. In 1960, Kittinger had set the supersonic jump record Baumgartner was now trying to break. Kittinger would be the voice in Mission Control talking the younger daredevil through the jump, step by step. Baumgartner was glad to have the colonel yammering in his ear. It helped keep his mind off that claustrophobic spacesuit. And if he ran into trouble, Kittinger's instructions might save his life.

SPIN CITY

Problems began on the balloon ride up. Baumgartner's visor fogged up. He still wanted to go ahead, so colonel Kittinger helped him prepare to jump blind. Once he reached 128,000 feet—the edge of space— Baumgartner unbuckled his seatbelt. He edged forward until his feet rested on a platform the size of a skateboard. "Stow umbilical," Kittinger instructed. "Stow *both* oxygen supply hoses. Stand up on the exterior step. Keep your head down. Release the helmet tie down strap. Start the cameras, and our guardian angel will take care of you."

At this point, Baumgartner's voice sounded a lot like Darth Vader in the Star Wars movies—

lots of heavy breathing with pauses between words. "Sometimes…you have to…go up really high…to understand…how small…you really are," he said. Then he saluted and jumped.

THIS MAKES MY BLOOD BOIL

Within seconds, Felix was spinning out of control in the thin air. The worst thing that could go wrong? The atmosphere above 12 miles (63,000 feet) is *so* thin that if his airtight suit failed, his blood would literally boil. "There's only one way for the blood to leave your body and that's through your eyeballs. That means you're dead," Felix said later. "It was terrifying. You don't want to die in front of your parents and all these people. I thought, please God, don't let me down."

As his body spiraled, Baumgartner's brain spun through the 40 different scenarios he'd discussed with Kittinger before the jump. That helped him regain control once the air thickened. He broke the sound barrier at 690 miles per hour (the speed of sound varies depending on altitude and other conditions). After 4 minutes and 20 seconds in free fall, Baumgartner pulled the ripcord and parachuted the last two miles to Earth. He landed on his feet in the New Mexico desert, knelt on the ground, and pumped his fists in the air. And then…he retired from the daredevil business.

"Trust me," he told reporters. "When you stand up there on top of the world you become so humble it's not about breaking records anymore. It's about coming home."

DARE-DEVILING NUMBERS

8 MILLION. The number of YouTube viewers watching Felix's jump, setting a record for a live YouTube event.

128,100 FEET. The altitude Felix jumped from, setting the record for the highest altitude skydive, highest jump from a platform, and the highest manned balloon flight.

119,846 FEET. The record for the longest distance for a free fall set by Felix Baumgartner on this jump.

102,800 FEET. Colonel Joe Kittinger's unofficial record jumping from a high-altitude balloon in 1960.

2,900 POUNDS. The weight of the customized capsule Baumgartner rode up in and jumped from.

833.9 MPH. Felix's maximum vertical speed during his plummet to Earth, making him the first human to break the sound barrier outside a vehicle and earning him the record for the fastest free fall.

807.2 MPH AT 43,000 FEET. Chuck Yeager's numbers when he broke the sound barrier flying his bullet-shaped plane on October 14, 1947.

300. The number of engineers, doctors, and other experts involved with the jump on the ground.

24 MILES. How far above planet Earth Felix was when he jumped.

5 YEARS. The time it took the Stratos Mission to prepare for Felix Baumgartner's jump.

70 BELOW ZERO F. The anticipated temperature in the ultra-thin atmosphere at the top of Felix's jump.

35 SECONDS. How long Felix spun wildly in the stratosphere before regaining control in thicker air.

GHOUL SCHOOL

....

Giggles and groaners for boys and ghouls.

Q: How do ghouls watch cartoons?
A: On a wide scream TV.

Q: Why did the ghoul stay home from school?
A: He was feeling rotten.

LITTLE GHOUL: Why do you get to stay up late on Halloween but I don't?
BIG GHOUL: Because I'm the mummy.

Q: What's on the menu at ghoul school?
A: Goulash and ghoul-aid.

Q: How did the ghoul's mom stop her from biting her nails?
A: By making her wear shoes.

GHOUL: My dog is just like one of the family.
TEACHER: Which one?

Q: How do ghouls like their eggs?
A: Terror-fried.

Q: Why didn't the ghoul finish his math test?
A: Because when he added four and four, he got ate.

Q: What do you do if a ghoul rolls her eyes at you?
A: Pick them up and roll them back.

Q: Why was the ghoul's mother so upset when he came home with a broken nose?
A: He couldn't remember who it belonged to.

SNAKE & SHAKE

. . . .

An Uncle John's original!

LAST NIGHT...
my king snake passed away.
I'd had him for two years.
I'm not the kind of guy that cries,
But—man—I shed some tears.

I buried him out back, down deep,
And spoke my parting words.
My dad said he'd be happy, but
I don't think my snake heard.

I could be wrong, though, 'cause tonight
My king snake came alive.
I watched him wiggle from the ground.
I watched him jump and jive.

He did a kind of crazy dance
Perched right up on his tail.
First he shimmied, then he shook,
And then he gave a wail.

I thought I must be dreaming, but
I gave myself a poke.

I shouted, "Ouch!" and after that
My king snake hissed and spoke.

"Lisssssten, Chad," he said to me.
"The timessss we had were fun.
"I'm ssssssorry I can't ssssstick around,
But, well, I gotta run."

I blinked and raised a hand to him.
I waved. "It's cool," I said.
He slithered off with one more twirl.
But—was he really dead?

This morning, I went out to check…
And—sure enough—he's gone!
And there are swirls and curlicues
Spread all across the lawn.

I think I'll keep his secret.
My parents have no clue.
But I know I'm not crazy…
My king snake knows it, too.

I guess I should have known that if
I named him for "The King,"
That dead or not, that snake would rock.
Keep rollin', Elvis…sing!

•　　•　　•

MONKEY BUTT

....

An Uncle John's Eerily Twisted Tale!

GERALD LIVED ON THE MOST BORING street in the most boring neighborhood in the most boring town in the world. That's why he found himself pawing through junk at an old man's garage sale one Saturday morning. But what else was there to do? At that very moment, Gerald spied something at the bottom of a box. He grabbed hold and yanked it out. "What the—" Gerald stared at the thing in his hand. "Is that a tail?"

The old man chuckled behind him. "Yup. And it's still attached to a monkey's behind."

"A monkey's butt? Gross!" Gerald dropped the tail.

The old man picked it up and ran his thumb along the tail's stiffened bristles. Then he looked Gerald right in the eyes and said, "It's magic."

Gerald eyed him right back. "Magic? Then what's it doing in a garage sale?"

"Well, well." The man nodded. "A smart kid, at last. Why *would* someone sell a magic object?" He leaned closer and waggled the monkey tail in Gerald's face. "It's three-wishes magic," he said. "And I've used mine up."

Gerald's eyes widened "Like in a fairy tale?"

"A tale…yes." The old man's eyes twinkled. "And a savvy young man like you could have this magic monkey's behind for a mere five bucks." He winked.

Gerald fingered the five-dollar bill in his pocket. "Three wishes, huh. What are the rules?"

The old man's eyes widened. "So, you've read the old stories! What do you know about three-wishes tales?"

"Enough not to buy that thing without hearing the rules." Gerald glared.

"Okay. Here are the rules: One—You get three wishes and only three wishes. Two—You can't use one of your wishes to wish for more wishes. Three—If you use a wish to undo one of your wishes, then you don't get *anything* you wished for. And no refunds."

Gerald handed over the five, and the old man handed him the monkey butt. A weird tingling went up his arm and settled in his chest. Gerald grinned. He already knew what his first wish would be. "I wish there was a water park in this neighborhood so I'd never be bored again." The tail twitched so hard he almost dropped it.

The old man's eyes saddened. "Haste makes waste, young man. But good luck."

When Gerald got home, his mom met him at the front gate. "Honey, I have something to tell you. It's Arfy."

"Is he okay?" Gerald asked. Arfy was ancient and couldn't see or hear much anymore. He smelled bad, and his fur was all patchy, but he was still Gerald's best friend.

"He got hit by a truck." His mom's eyes shone with tears. "The driver felt so bad, he gave me this."

Gerald stared at the slip of paper in her hand: LIFETIME PASS TO WATER WONDER WORLD.

"It's that new water park down the street," said his mom as if she had no clue it was impossible to build a water park in a few hours. "One of their construction trucks ran over Arfy."

"Where is he?" Gerald tried to push past his mom. "I want to see him."

His mom put a hand on his shoulder. "Dad buried him in the backyard. We want you to remember him as he was." Her head drooped. "Not the way he is now."

Gerald stared at the monkey butt clasped in his hand. What had he done?

That night, Gerald lay in bed unable to sleep. He missed Arfy. "It's my fault he got squished." He got up and took the monkey butt out of the sock drawer. He'd already used one wish. If he used his second wish to wish his first wish undone, he'd lose his third wish, too. What could he do? An idea popped into his head. He could wish Arfy back to life! "I wish Arfy was undead," he said. The tail twitched, and he heard his mother scream.

Gerald ran downstairs and saw a trail of muddy paw prints. Then he saw Arfy. Arfy's fur was even patchier. His eyes were hollow and his breath rasped, but Gerald gave him a huge hug anyway.

"I guess we were wrong," said Gerald's dad. "Arfy wasn't dead, after all."

But Gerald knew that wasn't true. The next morning, Arfy looked even worse. He smelled worse, too.

"We can't have him in the house," said his mom. "Take him with you to the water park."

Gerald patted Arfy, and Arfy's left ear fell off. "Um, sure," said Gerald. He got the tape out of the kitchen drawer and taped Arfy's ear back on. Arfy didn't seem to mind a bit.

But the people at the water park minded. "What is that stench?" "You can't bring that disgusting creature in here!" "That dog doesn't have fleas, he has flies!"

Gerald showed the gatekeeper his lifetime pass. "You can come in," said the gatekeeper. "But that mutt stays outside."

Gerald looked longingly at the water park. His wish had worked. There was a water park on his street, but he couldn't go in. And Gerald's mom didn't want Arfy at home anymore, either. He had one wish left. Gerald took the monkey butt out of his pack. The old man had said he was smart. Surely he could outwit a shriveled-up monkey's behind. Gerald looked at Arfy and sighed. "I love you so much, buddy," he said. Then he grinned. "And I wish everyone loved you just as much as I do."

The next morning at breakfast, Gerald showed Arfy the headline in the *News Daily*: INCREDIBLE ZOMBIE DOG LOVED WORLDWIDE.

From then on, Gerald kept a roll of tape on hand to reattach the parts that kept falling off his undead dog. Arfy didn't mind one bit. And Gerald always threw the monkey butt ahead of them as they walked to the water park. "Fetch, Arfy. Fetch!"

THE END

DEADLY WORDS

· ·

When it comes to death, everyone has an opinion.

"Death is caused by swallowing small amounts of saliva over a long period of time."
        —**George Carlin**

"There are worse things in life than death. Have you ever spent an evening with an insurance salesman?"
        —**Woody Allen**

"I don't fear death because I don't fear anything I don't understand. When I start to think about it, I order a massage and it goes away."
        —**Hedy Lamarr**

"Death has a tendency to encourage a depressing view of war."
        —**Donald Rumsfeld**

"Death is only a larger kind of going abroad."
        —**Samuel Butler**

"Death obsesses me. I can't really understand why it doesn't obsess everyone."
        —**J. K. Rowling**

"The leading cause of death among fashion models is falling through street grates."
        —**Dave Barry**

"I've never actually really believed death is inevitable. I just think it's a rumor."
        —**David Carradine**

"For days after death hair and fingernails continue to grow. Phone calls taper off."
        —**Johnny Carson**

ANSWER PAGES

Find Count Fartula (page x)
Count Fartula showed up 19 times in the book (pages
i, ix, x, 23, 49, 74, 85, 115, 120, 129, 138, 188, 222, 228,
and 288). If you found them all, you win Count Fartula's
Vapor of Doom. Here it is—*Pfhtttttttt!*

Who's Haunting Who? (page 24)
Here's the final scare…uhm, score: Craig is in the yellow
room, haunted by the Butler. Tyler is in the gray room,
haunted by Patrick. Jake is in the red room, haunted by
Henry. Drew is in the blue room, haunted by Lucy.

BOYS	RED	YELLOW	GRAY	BLUE
CRAIG	X	O	X	X
TYLER	X	X	O	X
JAKE	O	X	X	X
DREW	X	X	X	O

GHOSTS	RED	YELLOW	GRAY	BLUE
HENRY	O	X	X	X
PATRICK	X	X	O	X
LUCY	X	X	X	O
BUTLER	X	O	X	X

How to fill in the chart, clue by clue.
Clue 1 tells us that the Butler is older than Henry.
Clue 2 doesn't help yet, but **Clue 3** tells us that the
Butler is also older than Lucy. **Clue 4** tells us that Patrick

is the youngest. **Clue 5** gives us the first chance to eliminate a possibility, so X out GRAY in Craig's row. **Clue 6** tells us that Lucy does not haunt the red room (the ghost cries for *his* cat). **Clue 7** tells us that the Butler (the oldest ghost) haunts the yellow room, so mark that with an O. Cross out the R, B, and G on the Butler's line, and also cross out the Y for Patrick, Henry, and Lucy. **Clue 8** places Patrick, the youngest ghost, in the gray room. When we cross out the possibilities on the chart, we see that Lucy has only one room left that she can haunt: the blue one. That leaves the red room for Henry. Now we know which room each ghost haunts. (Henry=red; Butler=yellow; Patrick=gray; Lucy=blue.) **Clue 9** tells us that Drew is in the blue room, haunted by Lucy (because she's restless). **Clue 10** tells us Jake is not in the yellow room, because we know from Clue 2 that he chose the attic, and from Clue 7 that the Butler doesn't go up there. **Clue 8** tells us that the blue room and the gray room are across the hall from each other. That means neither of them is in the attic: Clue 2 told us that there's only one room up there. That puts the red room for the attic and that has to be where Jake is. That means Jake is haunted by Henry, who is in the red room. The only room remaining for Tyler is the gray one, so Craig must be in the yellow. Logical, yes?

Beastly Big (page 104)
1. C. giant beavers, **2.** A. saber-tooth cats, **3.** E. dire wolves, **4.** B. giant short-faced bear, **5.** D. the gigantic armadillo-like glyptodon.

THE LAST PAGE

FELLOW BATHROOM READERS: Bathroom reading should never be taken loosely, so Sit Down and Be Counted! Join the Bathroom Readers' Institute. Just go to www.bathroomreader.com to sign up. It's free! Or send a self-addressed, stamped envelope and your email address to: Bathroom Readers' Institute, P.O. Box 1117, Ashland, Oregon 97520. You'll receive a free membership card, our BRI newsletter (sent out via email), discounts when ordering directly through the BRI, and a permanent spot on the BRI honor roll!

UNCLE JOHN'S NEXT BATHROOM READER FOR KIDS ONLY IS ALREADY IN THE WORKS!

Is there a subject you'd like to read about in our next Uncle John's Bathroom Reader for Kids Only? Go to CONTACT US at www.bathroomreader.com and let us know. We aim to please.

Well, we're out of space, and when you've got to go, you've got to go. Hope to hear from you soon. Meanwhile, remember…

GO WITH THE FLOW!